W9-AYA-514

Understanding
Modern
Theology II

UNDERSTANDING MODERN THEOLOGY II

Reinterpreting Christian Faith
for Changing Worlds

JEFFERY HOPPER

FORTRESS PRESS   PHILADELPHIA

Biblical quotations, unless otherwise noted, are from the Revised Standard
Version of the Bible, copyright 1946, 1952, © 1971, 1973 by the Division of
Christian Education of the National Council of the Churches of Christ in the
U.S.A., and are used by permission.

COPYRIGHT © 1987 BY FORTRESS PRESS

All rights reserved. No part of this publication may be reproduced, stored
in a retrieval system, or transmitted in any form or by any means, electronic,
mechanical, photocopying, recording, or otherwise, without the prior permission of the copyright owner.

Library of Congress Cataloging-in-Publication Data

Hopper, Jeffery, 1930–
  Understanding modern theology II.

  Bibliography: p.
  Includes index.
  1. Theology, Doctrinal—History—Modern period,
1500–   . I. Title.
BT27.H673 1987   230'.09'03   87–12069
ISBN 0-8006-2050-X

2993D87   Printed in the United States of America   1–2050

To Jean

CONTENTS

INTRODUCTION

WE LIVE TODAY in a world that is profoundly different from that in which Saint Paul, Saint Augustine (354–430), Saint Thomas (1225–74), Martin Luther (1483–1546), or even John Wesley (1703–91) formulated interpretations of Christian faith. Yet a great many persons believe today that Christianity must be understood in terms of such premodern formulations. Some of these persons find great comfort in holding to those doctrines. Others reject Christianity because, seeing it in terms of the concepts and assumptions of other times, they find it to be incompatible with the world in which they live now. Modern theologians find both the affirmation and the rejection to be misguided. The affirmation, by trusting in specific human interpretations, gives a false, indeed idolatrous, security. The rejection, though right in repudiating that misplaced trust, is unsound and unfortunate, for it is not a rejection of Christian faith but only of those time-bound formulations.

This is not to suggest that the theologians named above failed to proclaim the Christian gospel. Modern theologians know themselves to be profoundly in debt to their interpretations. It is rather to recognize that for us to preach and teach today precisely as any of these past interpreters did would be to communicate something other than they intended. In order to convey today the meanings which they conveyed in their various premodern cultural settings, it is necessary to reinterpret.

In *Understanding Modern Theology I: Cultural Revolutions and New Worlds,* I sought to explain some of the cultural revolutions that brought about basic differences between the experiential worlds within which the traditional Christian orthodoxies were formulated and the world in which we live today and to indicate in each case the ways those revolutions challenged the common assumptions of those orthodox theological understandings. Although I dealt with a wide variety of subject matter there (the beginnings of modern science from Galileo to Newton, the beginnings of modern philosophy from

1

Descartes to Kant, more recent natural scientific revolutions in biology and physics, the origin and development of depth psychology, and the development of historical-critical biblical scholarship), the same basic questions for theology are raised throughout.

First, it was shown that all human understandings and interpretations—including those in religion and theology—are historically and culturally relative. We not only do not experience and understand our world in the way in which persons of any premodern world experienced and understood theirs, we cannot. Historical and cultural relativity has always been a characteristic of Christian theologies, but its *recognition* is a characteristic that distinguishes modern from premodern theologies. That this is the case and what its importance is for theology today is the subject of the first chapter of this book.

Perhaps the most dramatic difference between the premodern and modern experiential worlds is that the premoderns understood the events of their lives—both individually and collectively—to be in significant part the result of supernatural interventions by God and the devil and angels and demons, whereas moderns believe that the same events are to be understood in terms of natural laws. Much popular religiousness clings to vestiges of that premodern supernaturalism, but even here the experienced worlds are vastly different from those of our medieval and ancient ancestors. This general cultural change has forced the theologians to study anew the questions concerning divine agency. Given the recognition that God does not, for the most part, interfere "miraculously" in human lives or world events, how are we to understand God's role among us? On this question there is much disagreement among modern theologians. What is characteristic of modern theology is the judgment that this question must be faced seriously. Why and how this is being done is the subject of the second chapter.

The cultural revolutions examined in *Understanding Modern Theology I* persuaded citizens of the modern world that various conclusions that were proclaimed by the churches were not true. Yet the churches had assured their listeners that they taught on the basis of divinely given authorities. Foremost among these authorities was the Bible, whose authority was based on an *assumption* of divine *revelation*. This divine source of the church's knowledge was so much taken for granted that the nature and meaning of revelation were not topics of critical theological concern. When, under the impact of the several cultural revolutions, it was recognized that the Scriptures manifest the historical and cultural relativities of human traditions and authors rather than the supposed perfections of divinely given statements, it became necessary to ask just what Christian faith can mean by "revelation." There is much disagreement on this question among modern theologians, but there is general agreement at two points: first, this is an issue which must be taken seriously; second, the predominant traditional assumption that the very words and statements of the Scriptures are the content of God's revelation must be rejected. The reasons for this rejection and some of the more common motifs in modern reinterpretations of the nature and meaning of revelation are the focus of the first part of chapter 3.

It was inevitable that with the doubts cast on traditional church teachings, the discovery of the historical and cultural relativities of Scriptures, and the reexamination of the understanding of revelation, the churches' claims to teach on the basis of divinely given authorities would be called into doubt. Modern theology has had, therefore, to reexamine the bases upon which it reaches its conclusions. The idea that our questions can be settled by simple appeal to scriptural and traditional teachings is no longer defensible. The ways in which modern theologians seek to answer the question of the bases or authorities which ground their theological conclusions are the subject of the second part of chapter 3.

The cultural revolutions that have required modern theologians to recognize the need to reformulate Christian doctrines have also drawn greatly increased attention to questions of language and meaning. Language, the "medium" in which theologies are wrought, is also historically and culturally relative and inevitably ambiguous. Evidence for this has been forthcoming from modern science, philosophy, psychology, and biblical scholarship. The problems that have become apparent are particularly difficult in theology, because of the transcendent nature of its primary subject, God. How human languages, which have developed in the interaction of human minds and cultures with the finite objects of human experience, can be used to proclaim the reality and the will of God is another subject of much disagreement among modern theologians. An examination of the nature and importance of these problems and of some of the influential differing modern theological approaches is the focus of chapter 4.

The final chapter draws together the effects of these several areas of theological response to the modern world and summarizes the general characteristics of modern theology. Emphasizing how these characteristics differ from those of traditional theologies, this chapter seeks to show how precisely in these differences modern theologians today are trying to help the churches proclaim the same gospel that was proclaimed by the premodern theologians.

WORK CITED

Hopper, J.
     1987   *Understanding Modern Theology I: Cultural Revolutions and New Worlds*. Philadelphia: Fortress Press.

1
THE RECOGNITION OF HISTORICAL AND CULTURAL RELATIVITY

MEANINGS, UNDERSTANDINGS, AND relevancies differ from one cultural setting to another and change over the course of time within any particular cultural context. The phrase "historical and cultural relativity" is used to gather up a considerable variety of factors that contribute to these differences and changes. The acknowledgment of these relativities is probably the most common characteristic distinguishing modern from premodern theologies, and it has far-ranging implications that affect the very nature of theology.

Probably the simplest aspect of the historical and cultural relativity which affects theology is the continual changing of meanings of particular words. Consider, for example, this sentence from one of John Wesley's sermons: "Salvation begins with what is usually termed (and very properly) *preventing grace*; including the first wish to please God, the first dawn of light concerning his will, and the first slight transient conviction of having sinned against him" (LXXXV). Since the word "preventing" today means "hindering" or "stopping from occurring," an unwary reader might suppose that Wesley was making the point that our own initial religious impulses hinder the effective action of God's grace upon us. In Wesley's time, however, the word "preventing" had the prior and longer-standing meaning of "coming before" or "preceding," and it was commonly used in connection with "grace" to affirm the priority of God's graciousness. Thus in this case what Wesley affirmed was that even our first good inclinations in relation to God are not a result of our goodness but of God's free-loving action. Today, in theological discourse, the word "prevenient" is used where in Wesley's time (eighteenth century) the word "preventing" was commonly employed.

The factors involved in historical and cultural relativity as it affects theology are, however, much more complex and subtle than the changing meanings of particular words. Among these factors are concepts, assumptions,

4

prejudices, new knowledge, changing methods, differing contexts, and altered world views. These are entangled with economic, social, political, scientific, and technological changes as well as with linguistic, philosophical, and religious developments. Galileo's observations and their corroboration by other scientists required a rethinking of the relationships of the cosmos to God's intentions and actions, and the development of modern science in general led to both a serious questioning of traditional assumptions about how God acts in relation to nature and history and to the recognition of a need to rethink the long-accepted views of knowledge, what it is, and how it may be obtained. This in turn required the theologians to examine the meaning and nature of revelation. In all these matters, what had been *assumed* could no longer be assumed—by those who understood what was being learned. More recent developments in the natural sciences have pressed these same issues further and have required a rethinking of some of our most basic concepts such as "cause," "substance," "matter," "space," and "time." The basic building blocks of our thinking, including those used in our traditional theological formulations, have been found to need reinterpretation. Even at this foundational level, our world of understanding is not the same as those in which the major "orthodox" Christian theologies were formulated.

Further, modern psychologies, including depth psychology, have taught us to understand persons in ways that differ from the beliefs and assumptions about human beings in those earlier cultural settings. And, in yet another field, the development of historical-critical biblical scholarship has increasingly shown the need to take account of ancient languages, beliefs, customs, assumptions, and world views if we are to come close to understanding what the biblical authors intended to say.

In brief, then, all persons in every time and place understand and experience life in terms of world views which differ in varying degrees from those of peoples living in other historical and/or cultural settings.

ILLUSTRATIONS FROM THE HISTORY
OF CHRISTOLOGY

The purposes of this chapter are to illustrate the historical and cultural relativity of Christian doctrines and then to discuss the implications of this recognition for current theological thinking. It should be possible to illustrate these factors at work in relation to any and every doctrinal formulation, so the choice here has been to go to the very heart of Christian theology and give illustrations from some of the major points in the development of Christology, the attempts to interpret the meaning(s) of the affirmation that Jesus is the Christ.

The Beginnings of Christology

The last statement already entails an illustration, for the word "Christ" was a title whose meanings were changed by its application to Jesus (whether by the early church, as judged by modern scholarship, or [assuming "messiah"] by Jesus himself as earlier supposed and still argued by some). The Greek title "Christ" had been chosen by those who had translated portions of the Hebrew Scriptures into Greek as the translation for the Hebrew word which we transliterate "messiah." It is very difficult today to attempt to ascertain the meaning of this designation of Jesus as the Christ for the early Christians. A part of the meaning would have come for them from their understandings of the Hebrew expectations regarding the Messiah, but that in itself is a very complex matter, for it is evident that there were varieties of expectations. But "Christ" was only one (even if historically the most important) of many terms employed by earliest Christianity in the search for ways to understand and proclaim what had happened in this Jesus.

The reader may be puzzled that this should be described as a problem. For each of us today the terms or titles "Messiah," "Christ," "Lord," "Savior," "Son of God," "Son of man," "Son of David," and others all have the same general meaning, and that meaning is whatever our own understanding of the nature and the accomplishment of Jesus may be. This is natural and to be expected, but it will hardly do if we wish to begin to reflect carefully on the meaning of our faith. It has been shown that at the period of the development of the early Christian witness and the writing of the documents that have become the New Testament, these several christological titles had different and complex meanings arising out of distinctive linguistic and cultural backgrounds. It has also been shown that the uses of these titles for interpreting what had happened in and through Jesus underwent a complex development involving changes in linguistic and cultural setting *before* the writing of any of our New Testament books. For example, in the earliest setting of Christian witnessing, Palestinian Judaism, the titles "Son of man" and "Son of God" did not indicate divinity. This is true also of the Aramaic word *mari*, a title applied to Jesus which we translate "Lord." There was another word which we also translate "Lord" which referred to Yahweh, namely, *'adhon*. But our books of the New Testament were not written in the Aramaic or Hebrew languages or in the setting of Palestinian Judaism. Rather, they were written in Greek and (for the most part) in Gentile settings. Here the terms and titles and their histories and meanings are different.

Most readers of the New Testament today are interested in what the terms and titles used there mean in the New Testament and not in earlier settings. It is true that the backgrounds of the various terms do not *determine* their meanings as they were employed in early Christian witness. They did, however, *influence* those meanings, and those terms, with the meanings which they already carried, were the terms chosen by the early Christian witnesses. It would be strange to suppose that those inherited meanings had no bearing on the intentions of the witnesses and very naive to think that we can ignore those backgrounds and yet understand the New Testament well.

But there is another problem for New Testament readers today. When we read the New Testament, we commonly forget that we read it under the powerful influence of a long history of interpretations. These interpretations, which affect our understanding of the New Testament, arose in other times and places due to the particular circumstances of those settings.

For example, one of the important factors that led the early church to try to clarify the relationship of Jesus Christ to "God the Father" was the setting of early Christianity within the Roman Empire. It was customary (and politically useful) to require conquered peoples to worship the emperor. Since the worship of many gods was common, this requirement could usually be accommodated. The Jews had been able to gain exemption from this requirement, for it was clear that their religion allowed for the worship of only one God. But what were the Romans to make of this new sect, the Christians? They resisted worshiping the emperor and insisted that they, too, believed in only one God, yet it appeared that they worshiped both God and Jesus Christ. If they could worship the man Jesus, why could they not also worship the emperor? This question was—sometimes—a matter of life or death to the early Christians.

Some Christians today evidently suppose that this was a question that could be answered simply by saying that "Jesus is God." But from very early in Christian history it has been recognized that so simple an answer produces serious problems which begin with the clear implication that Jesus was not a real human being, that his life was a deception, and that his example is not relevant for mere humans such as ourselves. They also saw problems in the simple affirmation that "Jesus is God" in relation to Jesus' passion and death. Would it mean that Jesus did not really suffer? Or would it mean, instead, that God suffered on the cross? Both options were unacceptable.

As the Christian witness continued and spread, it encountered new forms of these questions about Jesus and his relationship to God and about this God who was being described as having acted decisively for the sake of humankind in Jesus Christ. As the questions developed, so also did the answers, and, inevitably, differing answers came into conflict with each other. The matter was so important to the Christian interpreters (after all, was not human destiny itself at stake?) that the various parties to these disputes declared one another heretical and proclaimed that their opponents were no longer a part of the church.

Cultural Relativities in the Doctrines of the
Trinity and the Incarnation

The Role of Changing Rulers

The influence of politics can easily be seen in the processes by which the great christological disputes of the early centuries of Christianity were "settled."

The first great ecumenical council, the Council of Nicaea, was called together by the emperor Constantine I. He was the first emperor to become a Christian, and he believed he had come to power by the aid of the God of Christianity. When he gained rule over the eastern part of the empire in 324 (until then he had been emperor only of the western part), he discovered that the Eastern churches were seriously divided by controversy over the understanding of the relationship of Jesus Christ to God the Father. In his view this endangered the peace of the empire, not only because of the seriousness of the opposition between the parties to the dispute, but also because it threatened God's favor for the empire. Failing in his initial efforts to persuade the disputants to agree to disagree amicably, the emperor called for a council of the bishops of the empire at Nicaea. He not only paid the bills and attended the council, but he presided, he participated in the discussions, and it was he who made the crucial suggestion to include the word *homoousion* ("of one substance"), declaring, in effect, that the Son is in all respects equal to the Father. It had already been clear that this term and this judgment were not acceptable to one of the major parties to the dispute, and the evidence available indicates that a majority of the delegates did not agree with the position taken here by the emperor. Nevertheless, all but two or three of the bishops voted for the Creed as rewritten to exclude any subordination of the Son to the Father.

It is very difficult to resist the judgment that the power of the emperor was the greatest single factor in determining this major theological issue. It may be argued that the fact that the struggle continued well after Nicaea and that the church reaffirmed the decision of that council (and has continued to do so) makes the question of Constantine's influence unimportant. Yet the course of the battle continued to show the importance of the imperial power. When Constantine came under the influence of a different theological advisor, his own view of the matter changed, and those who had "won" at Nicaea found themselves in trouble. The "final" settling of the issue, reaffirming Nicaea, came at a second ecumenical council called in 381 by a new emperor, Theodosius, who favored the Nicene party and position. Politics affected doctrine!

The evidence indicates that Constantine believed—at the time of the

Council of Nicaea—that the decision made there was made under the guidance of God. No one should need to be reminded of the extent to which history is littered with the tragedies wrought by rulers and leaders who were convinced that they were acting under divine guidance. The problem is, how is one to determine whose decisions are the result of God's influence? This is yet today a major theological issue, and it is very likely to remain so, for part of what is meant by the word "God" is a reality that transcends the creaturely and which, therefore, is beyond our methods of proof and testing. One may further note that during the course of history the decisions as to what represents "God's will" have commonly been in agreement with those who had the greater power to influence the decision.

None of that should be taken to imply that the wrong decision was made at Nicaea. It may well be that the best possible decision was made there under those historical circumstances. The aim here has been only to illustrate one factor of historical and cultural relativity influencing theology.

The Influence of Changing Concepts

The role of the imperial power is not, however, the most important element of historical and cultural relativity at work in the history of Christian doctrines. More important is the fact that the concepts which are employed for theological decisions and definitions are subject to changes of meaning over the course of time and from place to place. Continuing to use the same words and concepts tends to result, sooner or later, in either no meaningful affirmation, a misunderstood affirmation, or a different affirmation.

Once it is determined that a firm and explicit decision is to be made on a doctrinal issue (as it was determined in the instances of the early ecumenical councils by the imperial powers), that decision can only be made in the language and concepts in which the makers of the decision do their thinking and with the assumptions of the world view within which they experience life itself. The participants at these councils did their work in Greek and in Latin, working in part with concepts whose meanings had been forged by Greek philosophy.

The importance of this element of historical and cultural relativity for theology can be illustrated by a consideration of the concepts signified in Greek and Latin by words that have customarily been translated into English by the word "person." This term has been one of the fundamental elements of two of the most important theological formulas in the history of Christian theology. One of these is the formula for the Trinity, that God is *one substance in three persons*. The Latin, "una substantia, tres personae," appeared first in the work of Tertullian (b. ca. 145) and underlies the decision of the Council of Nicaea. The other formula is the famous affirmation concerning Jesus Christ, that he is to be understood in terms of *two natures in one person*. This too is to be traced to Tertullian as "una persona, duae naturae," and it has been used to represent the decision of the Council of Chalcedon in 451 answering the question concerning the relationship of humanity and divinity in the Incarnate Lord.

Christians have long been accustomed to talk of God as "One in three persons" and of Jesus Christ as "one person in two natures." However clear or unclear these doctrinal formulations have been, it remains the case that most Christians today would insist that God is to be thought of as "personal" and that Jesus Christ is to be affirmed as a genuine and undivided "person." It does not follow, however, that in these vague assertions Christians of today are making the same affirmations as those that were established as orthodox in the early church. In fact, it is clear that this is *not* the case.

Consider first the decision of the Council of Chalcedon:

> Therefore, following the holy fathers, we all with one accord teach men to acknowledge one and the same Son, our Lord Jesus Christ, at once complete in Godhead and complete in manhood, truly God and truly man, consisting also of a reasonable soul and body; of one substance [*homoousios*] with the Father as regards his Godhead, and at the same time of one substance with us as regards his manhood; like us in all respects, apart from sin; as regards his Godhead, begotten of the Father before all ages, but yet as regards his manhood begotten, for us men and for our salvation, of Mary the Virgin, the God-bearer [*Theotokos*]; one and the same Christ, Son, Lord, Only-begotten, recognized IN TWO NATURES, WITHOUT CONFUSION, WITHOUT CHANGE, WITHOUT DIVISION, WITHOUT SEPARATION; the distinction of natures being in no way annulled by the union, but rather the characteristics of each nature being preserved and coming together to form one person and subsistence [*hypostasis*], not as parted or separated into two persons, but one and the same Son and Only-begotten God the Word, Lord Jesus Christ; even as the prophets from earliest times spoke of him, and our Lord Jesus Christ himself taught us, and the creed of the Fathers has handed down to us. (Bettenson 1947, 72–73)

Many volumes have been devoted to the interpretation of this creed, which is given here only to show the fuller context of the terms central to our illustration, the terms related to "person." The English word "person" is traced back to the Latin *persona*, which was the translation of the Greek word *prosopon*. It will also be necessary to consider the Greek word *hypostasis* because of the importance of the phrase "one person and subsistence."

The history of the Latin word *persona* can be traced to its use for "mask," referring to the mask worn by an actor in ancient dramas to represent the role being played. Hence, the word came easily to refer to the role itself. It then came to refer to one's status or condition, in effect, one's role in life. Thus, in Roman law, a slave was regarded as having no *persona*, for slaves had no rights or citizenship, no status. It is this last meaning—and not just "mask" —which is intended in the creeds.

Commenting on this, J. F. Bethune-Baker insisted that ". . . the most important fact to notice is that it never means what 'person' means in modern popular usage. . . . It always designates status, or character, or part, or function" (Bethune-Baker [1903] 1951, 233–34).

The original term here was the Greek word *prosopon*. Like *persona*, it has a history of meanings which are unlike our modern notions of "person." In the New Testament its primary meaning is "face," used in a variety of literal and nonliteral senses, much as we use "face" today. It also is used to mean "countenance," "look," and "outward appearance" (Thayer 1886, 551–52).

Scholars who have studied the uses of this term in the christological debates associated with the Council of Chalcedon have noted two reasons why *prosopon* was not used alone but was supplemented by the use of the term *hypostasis*. First, *prosopon* was the word used by Sabellius and his followers to designate temporary personalities of the Father, the Son, and the Holy Spirit, a view which apparently excluded any eternal personal life in the godhead, and thus a viewpoint which the framers and defenders of the Creed of Chalcedon wished clearly to avoid (Bethune-Baker [1903] 1951, 105–6, 234).

The second reason is also a concern to avoid an unacceptable interpretation, this time due to vagueness. Patrick T. R. Gray explains that even Nestorius (chief defender of one of the unacceptable positions) was happy to affirm "that Christ was one *prosopon*, since that term had such a wide range of meaning as to be almost meaningless as a way of identifying a Christological position" (Gray 1979, 87). Therefore Chalcedon added the term *hypostasis*. Gray adds, "In fact, when Theodoret suggests here that *hypostasis* be explained in terms of the vague term *prosopon*, he is patently subverting the intention of Chalcedon, which was to specify the sense of *prosopon* by tying it to *hypostasis*!" (ibid.). In other words, the word "person" in the christological formula of Chalcedon is a translation of a Greek word *prosopon* whose meaning was so vague as to be of no help in settling the dispute. To clarify the intention, the word *hypostasis* was added, and the resulting phrase—in English—became "one person and subsistence." It was the second term, *hypostasis*, rather than the first, *prosopon*, which was decisive for Chalcedon.

Thus the christological formula which comes to us as "one person, two natures" was originally "una hypostasis, duo physeis." This formula encountered much resistance, for in the concepts of the time it was commonly understood that there could be no *physis* without a *hypostasis*. One of the clearer explanations of what was at stake here is found in John McIntyre's *The Shape of Christology*. McIntyre points out that the two terms here were understood by way of Aristotle's distinction of primary and secondary substance. A particular existing thing is a primary substance, and that is the use of *hypostasis* here. The species to which that particular existing thing belongs would be substance in the secondary sense, and that is how *physis* is understood in the christological formula. McIntyre uses the example "Tom Jones is human." The existing individual "Tom Jones" is the primary substance (*hypostasis*), and "human" is the secondary substance (*physis*) predicated of him indicating his species (McIntyre 1966, 87). Thus by definition, there is no *physis* without a *hypostasis*. In this example, there is only "humanity" insofar as there are particular human beings. Note that *hypostasis* itself does not mean "a particular existing human individual." The *hypostasis* refers to the existing actuality of whatever kind of thing is being referred to.

The problem, then, in speaking of the Incarnate Lord as two natures (*physeis*) in one person (*hypostasis*) was the apparent affirmation of one *physis* which had no *hypostasis*, and it was understood that that was not possible. But to affirm two *hypostaseis* would have amounted to affirming two Christs.

One of the defenders of the Chalcedonian formula, Leontius of Byzantium (ca. 485–543), offered what became the most attractive solution to this problem in the theory of *enhypostasia*. He accepted the understanding that there could be no *physis* without a *hypostasis*, but went on to argue that that did not require that every *physis* have its *own hypostasis*. As McIntyre puts it, ". . . he affirms, in line with the Chalcedonian definition, that the human nature of Jesus Christ has no *hypostasis* of its own. . . . In fact, it is a *physis enhypostatos*, an enhypostatic nature; it finds its *hypostasis* in (*en*) the *hypostasis* of the Logos" (ibid., 95). This may have solved the logical problem, but it meant that in Jesus Christ there is no human individuality. Indeed, quite apart from Leontius's argument, Aloys Grillmeier, probably the most respected of the interpreters of Chalcedon, concludes that ". . . Chalcedon leaves no doubt that the one Logos is the subject of both the human and the divine predicates." Further, "the person of Christ does not first come into being from the concurrence of Godhead and manhood or of the two natures, but is already present in the person of the pre-existent Logos" (Grillmeier 1965, 490).

What the scholars are making clear is that the explanation of the relationship of humanity to divinity in the Incarnate Lord, Jesus Christ, *excluded* human individuality. It is the divine Logos which was declared to be the "person" (*prosopon*) and the "subsistence" (*hypostasis*) of Jesus Christ.

It should now be evident that even though the Chalcedonian formula also said that Jesus Christ was like us in all respects, except for sin, the council was not affirming anything like a modern understanding of human being. When they described Jesus Christ as "one person, two natures" they clearly were *not* saying what the word "person" means to us today. McIntyre suggests that when Christians insist today that Jesus Christ is a "person," a "true man,"

> we speak of him entering into the human situation; taking to himself the sorrows, the broken relationships, the economic injustices, the political tragedies in which men find themselves; shouldering the burden of their sin; and so making it his

that he dies where they should have died the death that really was theirs. In taking human nature in this sense, he makes decisions; he senses the *délaissement* (abandonment), the utter loneliness of man forsaken by man, and the recovery assured to man who reaches that point of dereliction. (McIntyre 1966, 112)

It is interesting to note that the problems we find in trying to understand the early church's affirmations of "one God in three persons" and of Jesus Christ as "one person, two natures" are different in the two cases. In neither case did the early church mean what we mean by "person" today. This recognition entails problems for us in the case of Chalcedon's statement regarding Jesus Christ, but it helps to remove some difficulties regarding our understanding of the doctrine of the Trinity. To speak of God as "three persons"—as we understand the word "person"—conveys a meaning of distinct individual centers of consciousness and freedom in God, a view hardly compatible with the affirmation of the unity of God. There have been those who have insisted upon this view as constituting the orthodox tradition and the teaching of Scripture, but that was not, in fact, the teaching of the early church, for whom the words for "person" did not have this meaning, and no such doctrine is explicit in Scripture. When we understand that the word "person" in Nicaea's affirmation of the Trinitarian God did not mean what we commonly mean by that word today, the doctrine of the Trinity becomes *less difficult* for us to grasp and affirm. By contrast, when we realize that the word "person" in the Chalcedonian interpretation of Jesus Christ did not mean what we commonly mean by that word today, the doctrine of the two natures of Jesus Christ becomes *more difficult* for us to grasp and affirm.

Cultural Relativities in Theories of Christ's Work

The purpose of this discussion has been to illustrate the historical and cultural relativity of doctrinal formulations. Attention has been drawn, so far, to political factors, to terms, and to concepts. Something of the importance of changing cultural assumptions and world views can be seen by consideration of some major points in the history of the Christian church's interpretation of the "saving work" of Jesus Christ.

It has been a part of the tradition of Christian theology to distinguish the "work" of Jesus Christ from his "person." Consideration of the latter has been called "Christology" in the narrower sense, and the study of the former has been known as "soteriology," from the word *soter*, meaning "savior." In asking about Jesus' "person," the concern has been to understand what he was (and is). The question about his "work" asks what he did for us and how. Most Christian theologians have insisted that these two questions must be dealt with in relation to each other. They may be distinguished but not separated. And the history of Christian theology shows this to be true. The arguments about Jesus' "person" have entailed consideration of his "work," and vice versa.

Contrary to some popular impressions, the Scriptures do not "spell out" any single, clear, systematic theological theory of "the saving work" of Jesus Christ, and the history of Christian theology acknowledges this in the fact that there has never been an ecumenical declaration of an orthodox position on Christ's work. Certainly various theologians and groups within Christendom have argued that their soteriological views were the only correct ones, and in different periods of church history different motifs and theories have been dominant. Two of the most significant of these shall be examined briefly here for the purpose of noting how they illustrated the importance of historical and cultural influences.

The Atonement According to Gregory the Great

A pervasive and powerful aspect of the cultural context of the early church is strikingly expressed in the following description by S. J. Case:

> The sky hung low in the ancient world. Traffic was heavy on the highway between heaven and earth. Gods and spirits thickly populated the upper air, where they stood in readiness to intervene at any moment in the affairs of mortals. And demonic powers, emerging from the lower world or resident in remote corners of the earth, were a constant menace to human welfare. All nature was alive—alive with supernatural forces. (Case 1946, 1)

After quoting this passage, Jaroslav Pelikan continues, "with but very few adjustments of vocabulary in one direction or the other, that description of the relation between the natural and the supernatural order could have been recognized by Jews, Christians, and devout pagans in the first century. It formed the common ground on which the apologists for Christian doctrine and their non-Christian opponents stood . . ." (Pelikan 1971, 1:132). It was, inevitably, the presupposed context of experience within which the Christian interpretations of the saving work of Jesus Christ developed.

A prominent element of this world view in most of the early interpretations of the saving work of Jesus Christ is the role of the devil. One should, perhaps, say "roles," for the different theories interpret the devil's role in different ways. In one doctrine the devil is defeated in combat, and Christ is the *victor*. In another the devil is paid, and Christ is the *ransom*. In a third view the devil is tricked, and Christ is the instrument of that deception. In yet another, wherein Christ is the *satisfaction*, the devil is seen as having no rights, deserving of no ransom, not needing to be tricked. He is conquered by holiness, not by battle. Something of Christ the "victor" may be seen here, but the whole setting is now very different (Aulén 1931).

The version that dominated Western Christian belief from the seventh until the eleventh century was the one elaborated by Gregory the Great, pope from 590 to 604. This aspect of his manifold treatment of Christ's saving work is most fully developed in his long commentary on the Book of Job (*Morals on the Book of Job*) in which the indexed references to the devil cover several two-columned pages. F. H. Dudden judged that this work was the most popular textbook of Christian doctrine throughout the Middle Ages (Dudden 1905, 1:195–96).

The main points of the doctrine are as follows. Because of Adam's sin, humankind is under the power of the devil. This bondage is just, even though Satan is not, for Adam sinned of his own free will, and God had granted the devil this power. All persons, as descendants of Adam, are inevitably sinners deserving of death. Even the most righteous are doomed at death to enter the realm of Satan. It was God's purpose to free humankind from this captivity and to do so not by power but by reason. As long as the devil exercised his authority over sinners, he was within his granted rights. If, however, he should overstep this authority and take possession of a sinless person, he would lose his power to hold humankind captive. But there neither was nor could be a sinless descendant of Adam.

> But who might there be man without sin, if he was descended from a combination in sin? Thereupon in our behalf the Son of God came into the womb of the Virgin; there for our sakes He was made Man. Nature, not sin, was assumed by Him. He offered a sacrifice in our behalf, He set forth His own Body in behalf of sinners, a victim void of sin, that both by human nature He might be capable of dying, and by righteousness be capable of purifying. This One, then, when the ancient enemy saw after the Baptism, then directly fell upon Him with temptations, and by diverse avenues strove to insinuate himself into His interior; he was overcome and laid prostrate by the mere sinlessness of His unconquerable mind. (Gregory 1844, 17.46)

This victory over the devil would not have taken place, however, had Satan not made the mistake of trying to take possession of this one to whom he had no right. Gregory evidently enjoyed elaborating upon the theme of how this mistake occurred. For example, in discussing the verse in Job 40 which says of the monster Behemoth (in Gregory's version of the text), "in his eyes He will take him as with a hook," Gregory develops the image of Christ's body as the bait and his divinity as the hook on which the devil is caught.

> He was caught, therefore, in the "hook" of His Incarnation, because while he sought in Him the bait of His Body, he was pierced with the sharp point of His Divinity. For there was within Him His Humanity, to attract to Him the devourer, there was there His Divinity to wound; there was there his open infirmity to excite, His hidden virtue to pierce through the jaw of the spoiler. He was, therefore, taken by a hook, because he perished by means of that which he swallowed. And this Behemoth knew indeed the Incarnate Son of God, but knew not the plan of our redemption. For he knew that the Son of God had been incarnate

for our redemption, but he was quite ignorant that this our Redeemer was piercing him by His own death. (Ibid., 33.14)

In essence, the devil was tricked into taking possession of that to which he had no right. Christ as Son of God was sinless, so the devil had no right to take him. Christ as human could represent humankind, so the latter were set free by the devil's error.

Here, as elsewhere, Gregory believed that his interpretations were following those of Saint Augustine, but the differences are significant. Some passages sound very similar. "In the redemption the blood of Christ was as it were the price given for us (but the devil upon receiving it was not enriched but bound), in order that we might be loosed from his chains . . ." (Augustine 1963, 13.15). But deception is not the means. The overcoming of Satan is, for Augustine, not just by wisdom but by righteousness (ibid., 13.13–14).

The deception theory did not originate with Gregory, but with Origen. It was Gregory, however, whose elaborations and dramatizations of it were decisive for the belief of Western Christendom. For Augustine, such a theory was unacceptable as a violation of God's righteousness. For Gregory, there was no such problem. There is a difference in the understandings of righteousness and justice, and this is indicative of differences not just between the men, but between their times.

Gregory grew up in the much-embattled Rome of the period of the Gothic wars, seeing the final destruction of its old glories. He was educated in its subsequently inferior schools. Dudden describes the "science" being taught at the time as

a curious medley of serious arguments and mere fancies, of quotations of pagan authors and the Bible, of strange etymologies used as authorities for supposed facts, of deductions from observed facts and from figurative expressions of Scripture misunderstood, of old mythological stories and moral and spiritual reflections. Amid this collection of ideas we find much that is interesting now, much that was doubtless valuable then, but also much that is fantastic, and not a little that is ludicrous. (Dudden 1905, 1:77)

Noting that Gregory's unquestioning acceptance of traditional doctrines was "without solid understanding" (ibid., 293), Dudden draws attention to three important sources of Gregory's characteristic interpretations. One of these was Augustine, but with an important qualification. ". . . The doctrines of angels, saints, demons, penance, purgatory, and the last things, contain many Augustinian elements, though they are derived mainly from the popular current beliefs" (ibid., 2:294).

As this suggests, another major source

is the body of common popular ideas, some of which were inherited from paganism, while others had sprung up in connection with the ritual and practice of the Church. These ideas were as yet undefined. They were fostered in the imagination of the people, but not yet presented clearly to the understanding. They were felt rather than expressed. It was Gregory's work, however, to give shape to these vague conceptions, to define them with precision, and to restore them as doctrines to the consciousness of the Church. Thus we get the religious fancies of an ignorant clergy and laity expressed in dogmatic formulas; and the current conceptions of angels, saints, demons, miracles, penances, satisfactions, purgatory, heaven and hell, are all brought in to supplement the older theology. (Ibid.)

That Gregory's theology was so influenced by popular ideas is seen by Dudden as accounting in significant measure for the widespread and lasting impact of Gregory's teachings. He points out that Gregory was a missionary to "barbarian" and uneducated peoples, and that he had therefore to present Christian beliefs in simple form. Emphasis upon laws, rituals, supernatural beings, and rewards and punishments was appropriate and perhaps necessary for superstitious peoples (ibid., 2:291).

Dudden drew attention to yet a third element of the historical and cultural relativity of the theology of Gregory the Great, his training in Roman law. That legal system provided the model not only for Gregory's description of the duties of the Christian life, but also for the understanding of the relationships of God, Christ, humanity, and the devil. "God's dealing with mankind is resolved into a series of legal transactions, and Christ, the saints and angels, and the devil have all their parts in the legal process" (ibid., 2:291–92).

It should be evident that the beliefs of Gregory are not only unacceptable but grotesque in the view of theologians today, and that this is not just in relation to the then-popular "mythological" features, but in central dogmas and in pervasive characteristics. But modern theologians, recognizing the reality and the importance of historical and cultural relativity, do not simply condemn so influential a part of our history as wrong and irrelevant. Rather do they ponder the possible implications of Dudden's suggestion concerning Gregory's theology that "it was, perhaps, the only form in which the religion could have survived the Middle Ages" (ibid., 2:291).

Anselm's Reinterpretation of Christ's Saving Work

So also must modern theologians ponder the much more sophisticated interpretation of Christ's saving work which eventually superseded Gregory's. This was the teaching of Anselm of Canterbury (d. 1109), particularly in his *Cur Deus Homo* (Why a God-man?).

Anselm lived in a time of greater stability, culture, and learning than did Gregory the Great. Indeed, the modern historians who specialize in this period speak of "the renaissance of the twelfth century," judging that this period of significant advance began about the middle of the eleventh century. But the same historians make it clear that this period was much more akin to Gregory's time than to ours. This is graphically illustrated in the following account quoted by C. H. Haskins from a description by a Syrian physician.

> They brought to me a knight with an abscess in his leg, and a woman troubled with a fever. I applied to the knight a little cataplasm; his abscess opened and took a favorable turn. As for the woman, I forbade her to eat certain foods, and I lowered her temperature. I was there when a Frankish doctor arrived, who said, "This man can't cure them!" Then, addressing the knight, he asked, "Which do you prefer, to live with a single leg, or to die with both of your legs?" "I prefer," said the knight, "to live with a single leg." "Then bring," said the doctor, "a strong knight with a sharp axe." The knight and axe were not slow in coming. I was present. The doctor stretched the leg of the patient on a block of wood, and then said to the knight, "Cut off his leg with the axe, detach it with a single blow." Under my eyes, the knight gave a violent blow, but it did not cut the leg off. He gave the unfortunate man a second blow, which caused the marrow to flow from the bone, and the patient died immediately.
>
> As for the woman, the doctor examined her and said, "She is a woman with a devil in her head, by which she is possessed. Shave her hair." They did so, and she began to eat again, like her compatriots, garlic and mustard. Her fever grew worse. The doctor then said, "The devil has gone into her head." Seizing the razor he cut into her head in the form of a cross and excoriated the skin in the middle so deeply that the bones were uncovered. Then he rubbed her head with salt. The woman, in her turn, expired immediately. (Haskins 1957, 326–27)

This account illustrates not only the sad state of medicine and the continuing lively belief in devils, but, more generally, the fact pointed out earlier by Haskins that throughout the Middle Ages the supernatural world was more real to the populace than the natural world (ibid., 304–5). This was true also of scholars such as Anselm, and not just of the uneducated.

Anselm repudiated the understandings of the role of the devil in the drama of human salvation as interpreted by both Gregory and Augustine, but not because he doubted the reality and the relevance of Satan. Rather it was because in Anselm's understanding of the relationship of all creatures to the Creator, the devil had no such just right before God as those earlier teachers had believed (*Cur Deus Homo* in Anselm 1954, 1.7). The devil acted unjustly and could, quite properly, be overcome by God's power.

There was a need for the devil to be conquered, but humankind's bondage to Satan was not, in Anselm's judgment, the fundamental problem that called forth the saving work of God in Jesus Christ. That problem was, rather, that in Adam's disobedience humankind had dishonored God.

> Man being made holy was placed in paradise, as it were in the place of God, between God and the devil, to conquer the devil by not yielding to his temptation,

and so to vindicate the honor of God and put the devil to shame, because that man, though weaker and dwelling upon earth, should not sin though tempted by the devil, while the devil, though stronger and in heaven, sinned without any to tempt him. And when man could have easily effected this, he, without compulsion and of his own accord, allowed himself to be brought over to the will of the devil, contrary to the will and honor of God. . . .

Decide for yourself if it be not contrary to the honor of God for man to be reconciled to Him, with this calumnious reproach still heaped upon God; unless man first shall have honored God by overcoming the devil, as he dishonored him in yielding to the devil. Now the victory ought to be of this kind, that, as in strength and immortal vigor, he freely yielded to the devil to sin, and on this account justly incurred the penalty of death; so, in his weakness and mortality, which he had brought upon himself, he should conquer the devil by the pain of death, while wholly avoiding sin. But this cannot be done, so long as from the deadly effect of the first transgression, man is conceived and born in sin. (Ibid., 1.22)

There is another interesting facet to Anselm's insistence that humanity must make satisfaction for its sin. In answering the question as to why God could not simply have forgiven humankind, Anselm points out that God created humankind to fill the places left by the fallen angels. If humans were allowed to go unpunished, they could never be equal to the angels who have never sinned, and they could not, therefore, properly fill those places (ibid., 1.19). In addition, it was Anselm's conviction that the forgiving of sin without punishment would violate God's justice (ibid., 1.24). But there is no way in which sinful humanity can make satisfaction. In the first place, everything which we are, have, and do is God's and is therefore already owed to God. Second, even the smallest violation of the will of God, precisely because it is a violation of the will of God, is so serious that no loss can compare with it, and it should not be committed "even to preserve the whole creation" (ibid., 1.21).

On these terms, one can see that satisfaction could only be made by God, for only God is both sinless and not owing of all to the Creator. Yet the satisfaction must be made by humankind. It is we who owed this immeasurable debt, for it is we who had dishonored God. Therefore only a God-man could solve the problem.

If it be necessary, therefore, as it appears, that the heavenly kingdom be made up of men, and this cannot be effected unless the aforesaid satisfaction be made, which none but God can make and none but man ought to make, it is necessary for the God-man to make it. (Ibid., 2.6)

Thus did Anselm explain the appropriateness of the incarnation, why there had to be a God-man, and how the death of Christ wrought the salvation of humankind. Of many other subtle and—to many of us today—curious points, one more may be noted here. Anselm took up the question as to why the fallen angels (including the devil) might not themselves have been reconciled to God, and he explained that this was impossible, even in a manner like that in which humans were reconciled. First of all, the salvation of humankind presupposed the possibility of one of them making the satisfaction. God the Son Incarnate could do this, Anselm believed, for all persons are of one race, being descendants of Adam. The angels, however, are not one race, for they were not descended from one, hence even a "God-angel" would not be able to make satisfaction for them. Further, in their case, the Fall was not plotted by another, as ours was by the devil, so their satisfaction would have to be made without aid, which, however, is impossible (ibid., 2.21).

It should already be clear that Anselm's interpretation of Christ's saving work and its relationship to the devil, though it may be seen as an advance upon the deception and ransom theories that had preceded it, manifests a set of assumptions that are alien to those characteristic of our culture. It may, nevertheless, be helpful to underline certain aspects of that historical and cultural relativity that may help us to understand why—after an initial period of rejection—Anselm's interpretation became dominant, even constituting a major influence on the theologies of the Protestant Reformation.

It should be noted that the success of Anselm's theory is not due to its being the manifest view of the New Testament, for "satisfaction" is not one of the New Testament motifs in its presentations of Christ's saving work. Concepts and/or metaphors of sacrifice, ransom, redemption, propitiation, expiation, and reconciliation are all to be found there, but not "satisfaction." These various New Testament expressions are not harmonized, and none of them is developed into a clear and full explanation. It is the history of theology that has sought such explanations. The concept of satisfaction as a vehicle for interpreting the saving work of Jesus Christ has not been found before the work of Tertullian (who, like both Gregory the Great and Anselm, shows the deep influence of legal concepts). But, as Jaroslav Pelikan puts it, the "momentous consequences of the introduction of 'satisfaction' into Christian vocabulary did not become evident until later" (Pelikan 1971, 1:147). It was the elaboration of this motif by Anselm which had these "momentous consequences."

There are several characteristics of the medieval world view (assumptions, convictions, prejudices, etc.) in addition to its supernaturalism that are reflected in Anselm's atonement theory and which may therefore be judged to have contributed to its great influence. Among these are the views of honor and justice and the "collective" sense of family involvement.

The heinous crime of Adam, deserving of eternal suffering for him and for all of his descendants, was, in Anselm's view, that Adam had dishonored God. Such an emphasis upon honor seems strange to modern hearers. But, in feudal times, "the idea of personal honor and loyalty was a vivid moral force even in the most violent times" (Thompson 1959, 704). A knight could not break his honor without degrading himself and risking his salvation (ibid., 724). This was true, however, not only of knights. One of the illustrations given in *The Cambridge Medieval History* is of a tutor who "offered his life in atonement when his pupil refused to keep an engagement he had made for him" (6:804). No doubt this was exceptional conduct, but it is the conviction which we would note here, not the question as to how fully it was lived up to, for it is the conviction that undergirded Anselm's interpretation of "Adam's offense."

It is not, however, just that God's *honor* was violated, but that it was *God's* honor, for the understandings of justice in the Middle Ages included the firm belief that the seriousness of an offense was dependent upon the relative status of the parties involved. Justice was not "an eye for an eye and a tooth for a tooth," unless the offended and the offender were of equal social standing. This is illustrated in the fact that "the most infamous crime in the feudal calendar was murder of one's overlord, and it is the rarest crime to be met with in the middle ages" (Thompson 1959, 704). This was related to the honor of the vassal, and it had very practical reasons, but it is also related to a centuries-old assumption about justice. It is to be seen as early as a sixth-century Burgundian code concerning the *wergild*, a system for substituting payment for revenge.

> Then the guilty party shall be compelled to pay to the relatives of the person killed half his wergild according to the status of the person: that is, if he shall have killed a noble of the highest class, we decree that the payment be set at one hundred fifty soldi, i.e., half his wergild; if a person of the middle class, one hundred soldi; if a person of the lowest class, seventy-five soldi. (Quoted in Cook and Herzman 1983, 124)

When this understanding of justice is shifted from the offenses of persons against one another to the issue of the offense of a creature against the Creator, the result must be that the offense is infinite, beyond all measure and beyond any possible satisfaction by the creature, for the creature, who owes all to the Creator already, is finite, and the Creator, the one offended, is infinite. To be a traitor to one's overlord was judged to be deserving of torture and death. What punishment could suffice for offending the honor of God? Put in this way, one can see the "logic" by which eternal hellfire should have been affirmed. Pelikan describes these convictions—with particular reference to Anselm's teachings—as follows:

> In the moral sphere, the transcendence of God was his justice; for "when we say that God is better than man, we mean nothing other than that He transcends all men." Therefore man had to confess not only that "He is most high and I am weak," but also that "He is most just and I am wicked," thus expressing not only the awe of the finite creature in the presence of the infinite Creator, but also the

guilt of the sinner in the presence of the holy Judge. So just was God that the very presence of punishment was evidence of sin in the one being punished, since God could not condemn anyone unjustly. . . . "God cannot in any way do anything unjust." Although, in the eyes of men, infants who died before baptism had committed no sin and should not be condemned, God judged differently and condemned them justly, "not for Adam's sin but for their own." (Pelikan 1978, 3:111)

One may see here how the views of law and justice and the understandings of God were of mutual influence. The laws themselves were believed to have come from God, through Scripture and the church. They were not from humans, and therefore they were not properly subject to question by humans. Suffering in this life was judged to be deserved punishment from God and an expression of God's compassion because of its effects upon our eternal destiny.

Another assumption of the Middle Ages which underlies Anselm's theology is reflected in the practice of trial by battle. The practice itself reflects the conviction that God is directly, constantly, and justly involved in human events, for it is that supposed divine role which was the basis for the belief that the victor was the innocent party. For this reason, if the accuser lost, he (if he survived) and his family were to suffer the penalty which was otherwise in store for the accused and his family. It is this involvement of the families which I would emphasize here. A legal document from the Middle Ages which sets forth the proper procedures for such a trial concludes: "And if the defendant be vanquished, let the judgment be this, that he be drawn and hanged, or put to such other painful death as we shall direct, and that all his movable goods be ours, and his heirs disinherited; and his children shall be incapable of ever holding land in our realm" (Coulton 1928, 3:14).

The specific inclusion of the family, including children, in the penalties was related to an understanding of persons unlike the individualistic assumptions of more recent times. Nations and tribes were represented by their leaders and shared their fate. The members of families were seen as "participating" in a whole larger than the individual, and they therefore shared "the just rewards and punishments." This kind of understanding is to be seen in Anselm's interpretation of the representation of humankind by Jesus Christ and the possibility of his making satisfaction for all.

Because today's readers often do not struggle to understand the judgments and interpretations of earlier times in the light of the circumstances, customs, and convictions of those times, they commonly respond to Anselm's interpretation of Christ's work much as the following paragraph responds to the similar theology of Milton's *Paradise Lost*.

Further exacerbating the problem is the difficulty not only of Satan's very existence in the poem and his seemingly heroic opposition to the God of *Paradise Lost*, but also the creation and existence of Hell and God's rather severe treatment of Satan—even to the point of his damnation, including his involuntary metamorphosis into a serpent in Book X. In plain terms, either Milton's God is not so omnipotent as the poet wishes us to believe, and thus is incapable of exercising total control over the world He made, or if He is omnipotent, then He is surely not so just, good, and loving as Milton claims that He is. For no God of justice, goodness, and love would indulge Himself in such harsh and unfair treatment of any of His creatures or permit the existence of such wickedness and woe, clearly antithetical to His wholesome creation and to His loving purposes. (Hamlet 1976, 16)

It should be clear, even to those contemporary readers who share the views of this author far more than those of Milton or Anselm, that this kind of argument would have had no weight against Anselm. It presupposes assumptions and convictions that were alien to Anselm's culture. This is not to say that it would have been impossible for another creative theological thinker in Anselm's time and culture to have offered a very different interpretation of the saving work of Jesus Christ. Indeed, another such teacher, Peter Abelard (d. 1142), did offer a very different theory of the atonement, one which emphasized forgiveness and its effect on the inner being of persons (rather than satisfaction and its effect on the external relationship between God and humankind). It is a view that some Christian theologians in the modern era have found much more attractive than Anselm's or Gregory's or Augustine's, but it was not persuasive to very many in its own time. Anselm's view was.

THE THEOLOGICAL IMPORTANCE OF THE RECOGNITION OF HISTORICAL AND CULTURAL RELATIVITY

The foregoing discussions of some aspects of some major events in the history of the church's attempts to proclaim the good news of what God has done in Jesus Christ have been intended to illustrate the fact that every doctrinal formulation entails historical and cultural relativity. This fact has several implications for theology and raises some further questions.

The Relativity of Doctrinal Formulations

The first implication is the negative one, that no particular doctrinal formulation can be simply identified with the truth itself. This may well be judged to be true on the different and more important grounds of the transcendence and the graciousness of God, but that is not my point here. What I have tried to illustrate is that theological formulations are always developed and heard in particular languages, words, and concepts, that they inevitably entail the assumptions, convictions, prejudices, cultural values, and state of knowledge of particular peoples in particular times and places. Even if it is judged that the words of Jesus, insofar as we may have some confidence about which are truly his, have a special authority, it remains clear that those words also illustrate the linguistic, cultural, and historical entanglements we have discussed. In order for persons in other times and places who think in other languages to grasp and be grasped by their truth, several interpretive steps are necessary.

The Need for Knowledge of History

Clearly, the serious student of theology must also be a student of history, including but not being limited to the history of doctrines. Otherwise one may be sure to misunderstand the formulations of previous eras (including the Scriptures) and will be likely to make the mistake either of simply accepting or of simply rejecting those formulations. With the helps that have been provided (and are being provided) by the specialists who study the appropriate times, cultures, languages, and so on, we can get past the first impressions those teachings give us and gain some understanding of what they meant in their own historical and cultural settings and why they had such an impact that we are aware of them today.

Such growing historical understanding enables us to recognize how we have been influenced by these past teachings and thus gives us some critical perspective on our own assumptions and prejudices. Even persons who have never read any academic theology have, if part of some Christian community, been influenced by such doctrinal formulations as we have discussed through hymns, liturgies, prayers, sermons, stories, and other literature, art, laws, and customs, for we are part of a culture which has been profoundly influenced by the history and imagery of Christianity. Insofar as we remain ignorant of these influences, we naively suppose, for example, that we understand the Scriptures, failing to realize that what we assume to be their meanings are some other times' interpretations.

The Importance of Continuing
Theological Reformulation

A more positive implication of the recognition of the historical and cultural relativity of doctrinal formulations is that it enables one to understand one important reason why Christian theology has always been in the process of reformulation and, indeed, should be in such process. It is not the only reason and not even the most important one, but it is an inescapable one. To attempt to leave our doctrines in some supposedly unchangeable form would be to commit ourselves to a gradually increasing loss of the meanings those doctrines had and to require of ourselves an ongoing task of self-deception. These things have been attempted often enough in Christian history and continue among us today. The appeal of rigid dogmatism (especially in religion, ethics, law, and politics) always increases in times of great anxiety, for it seems to provide security. The Bible itself is a record of the struggle to over- come such false securities, and that iconoclasm (smashing of idols) is always one of the tasks of theology as it seeks ways in which this and other forms of blindness to God's grace may be outmaneuvered by expressions of that reality which slip past our anxious, self-protective defenses.

It is not unusual to hear a fearful objection to this recognition of the neces- sity of continual theological reformulation expressed in the familiar analogy of "throwing out the baby with the bath water." No doubt, when that anal- ogy was new, it had a considerable suggestive power. However, even then, it did no more that point to an important question, and it oversimplified that question in doing so. The problem is both real and important, but it is hardly simple. Put in these terms, theology is always struggling with the question, What is the baby, and what is the bath water? The first trouble with the anal- ogy is that it argues from a situation in which that question does not exist, for we know which is the baby and which is the bath water. There are indeed those who are firmly convinced that they know exactly what the truth of the gospel is, but what they illustrate in that dogmatic confidence is not faith and wisdom, but ignorance and idolatry. The facts of historical and cultural rela- tivity constitute one clear indication of this, and their recognition by modern theology is part of the effort to deal with the question about God's truth as distinguished from human formulations.

The oversimplification in such an analogy goes further, however, for it implies the possibility of a simple separation—in this context—of God's truth from those human and historical formulations. We can have the baby without the bath water, and that is exactly as it should be most of the time. But we cannot have access to the gospel apart from some kind of hu- man formulation.

It is not therefore to be regretted that there is always—in one form or another—an ongoing debate in theology between "conservatives" and "liber- als." These are, of course, vague terms, and they are often used with deroga- tory overtones and undertones implying such meanings as "stupidity" and "heresy," rather than their dictionary meanings. In the hope that those words are not lost to reasonable discourse, they will be employed here in their de- scriptive sense. The "conservative" concern is to maintain the achievement of past witnesses, interpreters, councils, and theologians whose work made it possible for Christian faith and community to survive other times, changes, and struggles so that even we might hear the good news. They insist that there is therefore something there which must be conserved.

The "liberal" concern is that we must be free to hear that good news as it most powerfully meets us here and now and free to seek new ways of ex- pressing the ever-surprising reality of God's love, and for this reason we must be free from the specific forms and limits set in the past. Surely both are, thus far, right. We can only be free from the past by being free for the past, and vice versa. If our freedom from the past is an ignorance and neglect of it, we will be cut off from our own roots and lose that freedom at its source. If our conserving of the accomplishments of our theological forebears consists of an insistence upon a sacrosanct status for their doctrinal formulations, we will miss the meaning they expressed both for their time and for ours. Neither the conservative nor the liberal in theology wishes to be understood in these ways. Their difference is one of emphasis. Their dialogue benefits the whole community which becomes the judge of the proper balance of their apparently competing concerns.

The Question Regarding the Nature of Theological Truth

One of the serious theological questions that arises in this debate, in part because of the recognition of the historical and cultural relativity of doctrinal formulations, is the question regarding the *nature* of the *truth* that theology seeks to express. In most aspects of our lives we have no reason to question the assumption that *truth* is a correspondence between a statement and an objective state of being. So I can say, for example, the sun is shining now, and anyone who understands our language and recognizes that I am using it in the normal everyday fashion will acknowledge that the statement is true. But if we ask whether it is true that God is just, we no longer have so simple a question. God is not available for perceptual verification in the way the sunlight is, and convictions about what it means to be "just" differ from person to person as well as from culture to culture—to mention but two obvious complications, both of which entail historical and cultural relativities. The question being raised here reaches further, however.

Suppose we ask whether Gregory the Great's interpretation of the saving work of Jesus Christ was true, or whether Anselm's was. No doubt there are those who are eager to say yes and others no, but neither sees the underlying question. Can it be assumed that theological truth (and that means, directly or indirectly, truth concerning God) is of such a nature that it can be contained in human statements? Or may it rather be the case that the kind of truth with which theology is concerned is "nonpropositional," that is, of such a nature as that it is never identical with statements. This is an old and a continuing debate among theologians. It arises in this context because the "nonpropositional" alternative is suggested by the illustrations given above of historical and cultural relativity in the teachings of Gregory and Anselm. At least this is so if we acknowledge the probability of the judgment that both of those doctrines did in fact help the church to maintain and to spread Christian faith. This was in spite of the facts that those two interpretations in part contradicted each other and that both of them are built upon assumptions about reality which most of us today cannot share.

The inescapability of ambiguity shows up in the previous sentence in the reference to "Christian faith." The point being suggested is *not* simply that people joined the church and accepted the doctrines of Gregory or Anselm. Intellectual belief is not what is meant here by "faith," but the more Pauline sense, which in the language of some of the Protestant Reformers (affirmed by many Catholic as well as Protestant theologians today) may be spoken of in terms of deep personal trust, reconciliation, and love. Did not the teachings of Gregory and Anselm help to bring about such faith, such lives transformed by taking the risk of trusting in God? It would so appear. Indeed, anyone who believes today that he or she participates in such a faith should hesitate to deny that those historic doctrines have helped to make this possible.

The suggestion of a nonpropositional understanding of theological truth would be that the truth is not in the doctrines themselves, but in the faith-relationship that those doctrines may help to make possible for some people. Thus, to continue to oversimplify, while to some of us today the doctrinal formulations of Gregory and Anselm may convey a contradiction to our sense of the grace of God, it is possible to see how in their own times and cultures they may have helped persons to take the risk of trusting profoundly in God —as, indeed, it appears they did. The truth or falsehood would not be in the doctrines themselves, but in the reality experienced in the faith or unfaith of the persons who responded to the preaching informed by those doctrinal formulations.

Such a conclusion would make clearer why continual theological reformulation has been and continues to be a characteristic of Christian theology, and why it should be. It would also modify the criteria in terms of which one attempts to assess both past and current doctrinal proposals, and it would help us to see how we can learn more from our traditions.

One of the things that can be learned from our traditions is that "continual theological reformulation" is not new. The history of doctrines is a record of such continual reformulation. A distinction has long been drawn between "doctrines" (a general term for "teachings") and "dogmas." The latter term has been employed to designate those doctrines which have been declared by the church authorities to be normative for the members. The decisions made by ecumenical councils at Nicaea (A.D. 325) and Chalcedon (A.D. 451) have had the status of dogmas. On the other hand, doctrines of atonement such as the teachings of Gregory and Anselm discussed above have never been declared to be dogmas by a larger authority of the church. Thus with regard to the larger portion of the teachings of the theologians and the churches there has been a recognition of openness for reformulation.

Even with regard to dogma, there has been an ongoing process of interpretation of the meaning of the authorized formulations. The kind of "dogmatism" which insists that specific doctrinal formulations are the truth and the only truth, though common enough, has not been well grounded in the distinctions of the theologians or in the facts of actual historical development.

The Fear of Relativism

The recognitions that all doctrinal formulations (including those authorized as dogmas of the church) are historically and culturally relative and the suggestion that the truth does not inhere in the doctrines but in the reality experienced by persons of faith tend to evoke a fear of "relativism." It seems to some that if we judge that no doctrinal formulations are themselves the truth and that doctrines which conflict with each other and/or which are formulated on the assumptions of world views that are alien to us may nevertheless be or have been effective ways of interpreting the gospel in their own cultural contexts, then it is implied that all doctrinal formulations are equally valid, which really implies that there is no truth in them. It should be noted, first of all, that modern theology's affirmation of the historical and cultural relativity of doctrinal formulations is not a judgment that all doctrines are equally valid, even when it is coupled with a nonpropositional view of theological truth. When it is argued that the truth is not in the doctrines themselves, it is also being argued that there is ultimate truth which those doctrines are seeking to express in a more helpful way for their own cultural settings. Thus, for example, Christian theologians who today argue that the doctrine of the two natures in Jesus Christ is not adequate and may be misleading for us are usually not arguing that a better conclusion could have been reached at the Council of Chalcedon, and they usually affirm that the formula of Chalcedon helped to keep the witness to the gospel alive in the face of competing interpretations that would not have done so. Relativism is not a necessary implication of the recognition of historical and cultural relativity, and it is not affirmed by Christian theologians.

The Inappropriateness of Dogmatism in Theology

Modern theologians do recognize (though their rhetoric does not always show it) that Christian theology should be more modest than it has been in much of its history. That dogmatism which says or implies that our way and only our way is the true or acceptable way of understanding the reality, the activity, and the will of God is clearly ruled out by the fact of historical and cultural relativity (which has helped us to recognize that it is more profoundly ruled out by the grace of God, though that statement may sound—ironically—dogmatic).

The Value of Recognizing Historical and Cultural Relativity in Theology

Still, the critic may ask why a theologian should bother to struggle with these questions once he or she recognizes that our situation is—in regard to historical and cultural relativity—essentially no different from those of Gregory and Anselm. Whatever future lies in store for humankind, the peoples of that future will in various ways understand life and reality differently from the ways in which we do. We cannot suppose that our doctrinal formulations will then be any more helpful than we may judge Gregory's to be now. We all live within culturally conditioned worlds, and none among us sees the truth as God sees it. How then is "modern" theology any different from premodern theology?

In response to this question, at least two things need to be said. First, in many important ways the situation of modern theology is like that of premodern theology, and the theologians of today should be delighted if they could believe that their interpretive efforts will bear a small fraction of the fruit borne by the theological work of such as Gregory and Anselm, all recognizing that any such fruit comes by the grace of God, though that is a phrase which will need more careful examination in a later chapter.

The second response is that in relation to historical and cultural relativity there is a very important difference between premodern and modern theologies, namely, that the reality of historical and cultural relativity is recognized—or at least far more clearly recognized—in modern theologies. That recognition means that modern theologians can quite consciously take the factors of such relativity into account in their efforts to understand Scripture and tradition and to reformulate for the present. It means that they recognize the need to be more modest, less dogmatic, more open to the theological suggestions of others, more seriously engaged in dialogue with other theologians, other Christians, other perspectives, and other disciplines, and more aware of the dangers of idolatry lurking about the theological and religious worlds. For the recognition of the fact of historical and cultural relativity helps one to realize that real confidence cannot come from placing radical trust—even implicitly—in our doctrines. Such trust belongs only to God, and God remains transcendent.

This last affirmation shows the difficulty—the impossibility—of keeping issues of "method" in theology separate from questions of content. Historical and cultural relativity is a matter of neutrally observable fact, but the judgment as to just how it affects the theological enterprise depends in significant measure upon one's whole understanding of our faith. This probably shows up most clearly in the question concerning how we should understand the "activity" of God among us. That is the subject of the next chapter.

WORKS CITED

Anselm, Saint
1954   *Proslogium; Monologium; An Appendix in Behalf of the Fool by Gaunilon; and Cur Deus Homo.* Translated by S. N. Deane. Reprint ed. LaSalle, Ill.: Open Court.

Augustine, Saint
1963   *The Trinity.* Translated by Stephen McKenna, C.SS.R. In *The Fathers of the Church*, editorial director R. J. Deferrari. Washington, D.C.: Catholic University of America Press.

Aulén, Gustaf
1931   *Christus Victor: An Historical Study of the Three Main Types of the Idea of the Atonement.* Translated by A. G. Herbert. London: SPCK.

Bethune-Baker, J. F.
1951   *An Introduction to the Early History of Christian Doctrine: To the Time of the Council of Chalcedon.* 9th ed. London: Methuen & Co.

Bettenson, H., ed.
1947   *Documents of the Christian Church.* New York and London: Oxford University Press.

Case, S. J.
1946   *The Origins of Christian Supernaturalism.* Chicago: University of Chicago Press.

Cook, W. R., and R. B. Herzman
1983   *The Medieval World View.* New York: Oxford University Press.

Coulton, G. G.
1928 [1910]   *Life in the Middle Ages.* Cambridge: Cambridge University Press.

Dudden, F. H.
1905   *Gregory the Great: His Place in History and Thought.* 2 vols. New York: Russell & Russell.

Gray, P. T. R.
1979   *The Defense of Chalcedon in the East (451–553).* Leiden: E. J. Brill.

Gregory the Great
1844   *Morals on the Book of Job.* Oxford: John Henry Parker.

Grillmeier, Aloys, S.J.
1965   *Christ in Christian Tradition: From the Apostolic Age to Chalcedon (451).* Translated by J. S. Bowden. New York: Sheed & Ward.

Hamlet, D. M.
1976   *One Greater Man: Justice and Damnation in Paradise Lost.* Lewisburg, Pa.: Bucknell University Press.

Haskins, C. H.
1957 [1927]   *The Renaissance of the Twelfth Century.* New York: World Publishing.

McIntyre, J.
    1966   *The Shape of Christology.* Philadelphia: Westminster Press.

Pelikan, J.
    1971   *The Christian Tradition: A History of the Development of Doc-
                        trine.* Vol. 1: *The Emergence of the Catholic Tradition (100–600).*
                        Chicago: University of Chicago Press.

    1978   *The Christian Tradition: A History of the Development of Doc-
                        trine.* Vol. 3: *The Growth of Medieval Theology (600–1300).*
                        Chicago: University of Chicago Press.

Tanner, J. R., C. W. Previté-Orton, and Z. N. Brooke, eds.
    1929   *The Cambridge Medieval History.* Vol. 6: *Victory of the Papacy.*
                        New York: Macmillan Co.

Thayer, J. H., trans.
    1886   *A Greek-English Lexicon of the New Testament: Being Grimm's
                        Wilke's Clavis Novi Testamenti.* New York: American Book
                        Company.

Thompson, J. W.
    1959 [1928]   *Economic and Social History of the Middle Ages.* Vol. 2. New
                        York: Frederick Ungar.

Wesley, J.
    1860   *The Works of the Rev. John Wesley, A.M.* 5th ed. Vol. 7. Lon-
                        don: John Mason.

2

REEXAMINING HOW
GOD "ACTS"

THE STRUGGLES TO understand the roles of God in nature, history, and individual lives are not new, but they are different in the modern era. It was recognized in the ancient and medieval worlds that belief in an all-powerful deity entailed serious questions regarding both the vast amount of suffering and the affirmation of human freedom and moral responsibility. But the beliefs in the omnipotence and goodness of God were so firmly entrenched as to provide the bases for dealing with those questions. If a natural disaster destroyed many lives, it did not lead to doubt concerning God's power or character so much as raise a question about why those people were being punished. And it was a clear supposition of the scriptural writings that persons had sufficient moral freedom and responsibility to be subject to the judgment of deserving such punishment. So how God could be in direct control of all events yet neither be the perpetrator of evil nor interfere with human freedom could be regarded as truth beyond human comprehension, that is, as "mystery."

The enormous and growing impact of the developing natural sciences on the peoples who have benefited therefrom during the last two centuries has carried with it the conviction that nature operates in accordance with "laws." This basic presupposition of the whole natural scientific enterprise has been justified by continuing discoveries and accomplishments. It includes recognition of limits to human knowledge and understanding, but it is in severe tension with the popular notion of "miracles" according to which it is supposed that God "intervenes," displacing, setting aside, or overwhelming the normal causal relationships in order to bring about effects or events that cannot be accounted for in terms of the laws of nature, human freedom, and any other factors which would ordinarily be at work. In the ancient and medieval worlds it was "natural" to believe that a plague was the result of such supernatural causal intervention. No doubt there are many persons today who will both pray for a miraculous cure *and* seek the help of modern medical science when threatened by disease, but medical science progresses by trusting in the utter consistency of natural law. When a new threat to life and health such as AIDS is identified, the citizens of the developed nations expect medical research to search for (and sooner or later to find) the causes and cures or effective means of prevention, and they are willing—sometimes eager—to invest substantial sums of their money in this process.

There is an implication in this and the comparable procedures of the other sciences that we live in a world which does not suffer supernatural causal interventions. There has been much argument as to whether or not natural science and belief in divine intervention are compatible with each other, but it is clear that increasing numbers of persons have come to the conviction that the world operates without "miracles." This is a major cultural change, and it is in response to it that the question as to "how God acts" is a serious concern of modern theology.

As much of this chapter will seek to show, the question for the theologians is not *whether* God acts but *how*. It is a "given" for theology not only that God *is* but also that God's being, nature, and will are of the greatest possible relevance for human beings, and it is extremely difficult to imagine a way in which that could be true while also holding that God is in no way "active" in human affairs.

It is not difficult to understand why those "modern" theologians who seek to interpret Christian faith without appeals to supernatural causal intervention have been accused of arguing that God is utterly inactive in the affairs of the world. Ironically, one source of this hasty judgment is the impact of modern science, for it has encouraged the impression that there are only the two possibilities: either an agent acts "causally" or not at all. As discussed in *Understanding Modern Theology I*, more recent scientific developments have called in question the adequacy of the concept of "cause" which is implicit in this dichotomy, but because those developments are very difficult for nonspecialists to understand, the earlier scientific world view with its mechanistic character is still more influential in the general populace than is the newer one.

The tendency, however, to reduce the possibilities for understanding the activities of God among us to that simple alternative (either "causally" or not at all) is probably rooted more in the anxiety produced by the recognition of the degree to which the more traditional interpretations of Christian faith are cast in doubt by the questioning of the assumption of supernatural causal interventions. That degree is indeed very great. It is not only that belief in the inerrancy of Scripture and/or the unquestionable authority of certain teachings of tradition presuppose such interventions, for so also do those most characteristic and central Christian doctrines, the incarnation and the resurrection. Indeed, it is probably safe to say that the whole of Christian doctrine as received from tradition is built on the assumption of supernatural causal intervention. Hence, though one might say that of course those traditional doctrinal formulations were set forth in terms of this as well as other elements of the historical and cultural relativity of the ancient and medieval worlds, that observation does nothing to remove the appearance of a rejection of Christian faith itself with any surrendering of so important an aspect of its traditional interpretations.

One of the characteristics of modern theology is that where real or apparent conflicts arise between our culture's experience of the world and our interpretations of our faith, it is part of the theological task to probe those conflicts, assess their genuineness and seriousness, and make such judgments as whether Christian faith requires a repudiation of the modern cultural conviction(s) or whether the understanding of that faith can be modified (reinterpreted) in a way that removes the conflict with human experience without surrendering anything essential to faith's affirmations. This task is assuredly complex and difficult, but that hardly means that the responsibility can be avoided. To be sure, one might question the assertion that this is a characteristic of modern theology, for it can now be seen to have been a characteristic of the whole history of Christian theology. It is, however, more pronounced today for a variety of reasons, including the recognition of historical and cultural relativity, the greatly increased pace of cultural change, and the greater degree to which the cultural assumptions presupposed in our traditional theological formulations are challenged by our "modern world."

Within that general characteristic of modern theology is the more specific characteristic of concern with the question concerning "how God acts." This is not to say that all or even most "modern" theologians repudiate supernatural causal intervention, for that is not the case. What is being said is that, increasingly, the theologians are grappling with this question, recognizing that the traditional assumption of divine interventions at least appears to be in conflict with current experience and knowledge of the world in which we live and that the continued insistence upon traditional interpretations of Christian faith may be alienating many persons from that faith while it is also alienating many Christians from the modern world. It is difficult today to judge which is greater: the number of persons who affirm Christianity because they believe it to be wed to an earlier world view or the number of persons who reject Christianity for exactly the same reason. Modern Christian theologians may differ in their proposals for understanding how God acts, but they agree in the judgment that both of these groups are mistaken. By sketching some of the ways in which modern theologians are proposing to interpret the activity of God in nature, history, and individual human lives in light of the current knowledge and experience of the world in which we live, I intend to show that Christian faith is not a mere relic of our cultural history.

FRIEDRICH SCHLEIERMACHER: GOD, KNOWN IN RELIGIOUS EXPERIENCE, IS NOT A BUNGLER

These concerns are already evident in the work of Friedrich Schleiermacher (1768–1834), who has been called the father of modern Protestant theology. This is certainly not to suggest that Schleiermacher was the first to reformulate an understanding of God in light of the general impact of modern science and the accompanying cultural developments. There was already a long history of such reinterpretations among the philosophers. The seventeenth-century Deists, for example, had been very influential among the more educated in their depiction of a God who is knowable by reason unaided by revelation and who is understood to have created the world and left it to operate without interference in accordance with its own laws. Belief in "natural law" preceded the modern era, but the meaning of this phrase had changed. Throughout most of the history of Christianity nature was believed to be good and reasonable in spite of its mysteriousness because of the belief in the goodness and reasonableness of the Creator. Indeed, "natural laws" were understood to have their being essentially in the mind of God. They were not descriptions of nature itself derived from careful observation, but that is what the phrase had come to mean in the eighteenth century. In the earlier periods conclusions about nature were derived from convictions about God. Now, in the seventeenth and eighteenth centuries, conclusions are being reached about God on the basis of observations of nature. Among the evidences of the influence of such "natural religion" is the American Declaration of Independence with its appeal to "the laws of nature and nature's God."

This confidence in the reasonableness of nature and the possibility of inferring the reality and nature of "nature's God" from the observed "laws of nature" had already been powerfully refuted in the work of David Hume. His arguments against natural religion were of no comfort to supporters of the traditional interpretations of Christianity, however, for Hume found the appeals to such miracles as revelation even less compatible with the new methods of gaining knowledge, and he argued that we simply have no knowledge concerning God. Immanuel Kant, who said that he was awakened by Hume from his dogmatic slumber, sought to provide a basis for claims of knowledge in science and a foundation for morality while adding to the attack upon natural theology. He said that he had destroyed knowledge in order to make room for faith. This "faith," however, was strictly a matter of the intellect. It

was of the character of beliefs which the mind consciously affirms and not to
be likened to a personal relationship of trust and love.

All such philosophies of the Enlightenment were firmly repudiated as heretical by representatives of the churches. The traditional interpretations of
Christianity were reasserted by appeals to the authorities of Scripture, tradition, and church—all allegedly rooted in God's authority. These assertions
were no doubt well received by many of "the faithful," but for those who
were imbued with the spirit of modern science it was clear that such arguments simply begged the question. They defended a supernaturalistic understanding of the world by claiming supernatural authorities. There is no
discussion here. One side begins with a conviction that there are causal interventions and defends that belief by appealing to it. The other side simply
does not believe that there are any such interventions, believing instead that
the world operates in accordance with natural laws discoverable by scientific
methods, and allows only those methods as a means of testing any explana-
tory claims. This also begs the question, assuming the very point which is being disputed. To this day there are representatives of both of these positions,
who not only fail to recognize the unreasonableness of their alleged arguments but also continue to suppose that there *are* only two possible positions!
From its beginnings, however, what we today call "modern theology" has
sought to affirm *both* modern science with its conviction that the world operates with the regularity and coherence which make scientific learning possible
and the meaningful presence and activity of God within that world.

In Schleiermacher's judgment, both those who believed that there is no
God who is active in the world and those who defended the traditional doctrines of a God who intervenes and displaces the regularities of nature begin
with the same mistaken view of God, a view which implicitly understands
God in the same way that it understands finite beings. Certainly traditional
theologies have denied this, but in Schleiermacher's judgment they fall into
this trap by construing God's causal efficacy in the same fashion as they understand other causal efficacies. To see God as displacing or overriding or
supplementing natural causes (including human ones) is to think of God in
the terms appropriate to creatures, to reduce God to the status of a creature.
The naturalists, in denying the reality of God, were denying the reality of a
mistaken idea of God. The Deists, in denying interventions by God, were al-
lowing only for a finite Creator God alongside of nature because a "God" who
can be established by finite reason must be finite, and because science, which
can find only finite causes, found no clear evidence of supernatural interventions. The traditional theological views affirmed a finite intervening God,
construing God's role as another set of temporal and spatial causes, even if
more powerful and mysterious, where "mysterious" means something that
cannot be explained because it violates the laws of nature. All of this finitiz-

ing and anthropomorphizing of God, Schleiermacher argued, basically misunderstands what faith means in affirming the reality of God.

The traditional supernaturalists erred not only in this implicit reduction of
God to the status of a creature, however. In interpreting God's activity as supernatural causal intervention, they were, Schleiermacher insisted, declaring
God to be imperfect in some way (Schleiermacher 1928, 179). Indeed, as
R. R. Williams puts Schleiermacher's point, they were describing God as "a
bungler who must keep correcting his previous mistakes . . ." (Williams,
1978, 91). In so arguing, Schleiermacher recognized that his reasoning was
directly contrary to the view that miracle (understood as supernatural causal
intervention) is evidence of God's omnipotence. Rather, he held, it is the case
that the need to disrupt the regularities of nature which God had established
could only suggest either some inadequacy in God's creative and sustaining
work or some outside source of resistance to God's purposes. Either alternative would contradict the greatness of God which the defenders of miracle
suppose they are proclaiming (Schleiermacher 1928, 179).

This reinterpretation of the implications of "miracle" can be seen as a clear
indication of the change in historical-cultural setting. In the ancient and
medieval worlds, where openness to the incursions of many and various supernatural powers was the norm, God was praised by this attribution of yet-
greater intervening power than that of the other "powers." When the world is
understood in terms of natural law (and not supernatural powers), however,
to claim supernatural causal intervention by God may be judged to describe
God as in conflict with God's own creative work, and to imply that God is arbitrary, even capricious, rather than utterly trustworthy. (Of course, not all
modern theologians agree with these judgments.)

It would, however, be a serious mistake to suppose that Schleiermacher's
arguments against the concept of God as a reality alongside the world who
sometimes intervenes in its regularities and disrupts its natural laws are simply and solely a result of his acceptance of a "scientific world view." In order
to grasp the nature and meaning of his arguments it is necessary to see them
in the context of his basic theological perspective.

Schleiermacher's way of denying that God acts by causal interventions
while affirming that God is actively at work in creation is rooted in his basic
conception of the way in which God and the world are related. That judgment is not just another speculative conception, for it is grounded in Schleiermacher's conviction regarding the nature of religious experience.

Human religious experience is not a matter of dogmas that one believes or
of moral precepts that one obeys. It is, rather, immediate experience of God's
presence. The word "immediate" here is intended to indicate that this experience is not that of a subject apprehending an object. It is prior to or more
basic than such "over-againstness." Religion or piety is thus not primarily a

matter of knowing or doing, but of "feeling." This most basic and pervasive aspect of all human experience Schleiermacher called "the feeling of absolute dependence."

Schleiermacher's choice of the word "feeling" has contributed to much
misunderstanding, for that word easily suggests something "merely psychological," superficial, subjective, and irrational. But Schleiermacher's writings were clear that such was not his meaning. It is a sense of being a self in
relation to that upon which one is absolutely dependent, that is, of being in
relation to God. It includes a prereflective consciousness that all of our spon-
taneity comes from a source other than ourselves, and this "Whence" is called
"God" (ibid., 16).

Schleiermacher was so insistent upon this priority and otherness of God
that it is difficult to understand why he has so often been accused of being a
"pantheist." In these charges the word "pantheism" is used in the simplistic
sense which identifies God with the sum total of everything that is. Evidently
many persons in our cultural traditions are so immersed in subject-object
thinking that they cannot escape the assumption that for something *to be* it
must be an object or a distinct "thing." Schleiermacher was not just denying
that God is an object for our knowing, but also that God can be thought of as
a reality existing alongside other realities. But this was clearly intended neither to deny God's being nor to *identify* God with the cosmos. Rather it was to
insist that God transcends the limited and conditioned mode of being of all
particular realities—including the whole cosmos. In our feeling of absolute
dependence there is an implicit recognition that that upon which we are utterly dependent is absolutely dependable. It is therefore not limited or conditioned. Its transcendence of such creaturely status includes the possibility of
its immanence among all creatures. Because God is fundamentally different
in kind from all else, God can be intimately and profoundly present in, with,
and to all finite realities.

This way of interpreting the reality of God rejects as a false dichotomy the
view that either God is a reality alongside creation or else God is identical
with reality. Certainly these are two views that we can more readily imagine
and comprehend, but Schleiermacher (like others before and since) judged
that both of those views—in making God imaginable and definable—have
reduced God to a finite and conditioned status that is contrary to our feeling
of absolute dependence in which we have the immediate experience of the divine presence as that upon which we are utterly dependent and in which we
can place total faith. Thus a properly developed and understood religious
consciousness recognizes that God is both immanent and transcendent and
that God's infinite being somehow "includes" finite being.

When expressed this simply, Schleiermacher's views sound like a "natural theology," a doctrine of God derived by reasoning from generally available data. There are at least two basic reasons why this must be judged a misunderstanding. First, Schleiermacher insisted that there is a particular historical character to every religious experience. We may talk about religion in general, but there is no such thing. One's actual religious experience is always conditioned by historical and social factors. Schleiermacher was a member of the Christian community and held that Christian piety can only arise in some connection with the more specific religious experience that received its decisive impulse in Christ (ibid., 44). Second, the distinction of "natural theology" and "revealed theology"—as usually construed—presupposes the view of God as outside and alongside the cosmos so that there might be independent rational inferences from within "the natural world" and supernatural revelations from without. Schleiermacher argued against this whole way of thinking, proposing a perspective for which the distinction of natural theology and revealed theology is inappropriate.

The basis for the previously noted arguments against supernatural causal intervention should now be a little clearer. To think of God as a reality alongside the cosmos acting upon it from outside is to finitize God, to reduce God to the status of another finite being, even if the greatest. To be "the greatest" is to be comparable to those in relation to which one is "greatest." But religious experience, Schleiermacher argued, includes implicit recognition of the unconditioned or infinite dependability of God. Further, to suppose that God interferes with the regularities of nature is to think of God as having been unable to carry out the divine will in its creative activity. God is thus construed as being finite, limited, bungling, arbitrary, and even in self-conflict, contrary to Christian faith's certainty of the dependability of the love known in the experience of redemption through Christ (ibid., 56, 68–76).

To summarize Schleiermacher's position in this way is to raise at least two basic questions: (1) In thoroughly rejecting supernatural causal intervention, just what understanding of God's activity is Schleiermacher affirming? (2) How can Schleiermacher insist upon the decisiveness of God's activity in Jesus Christ without returning to supernatural causal intervention?

The answer to the first question is already implicit in what has been said. In humankind's feeling of absolute dependence there is an intuitive experience of God's living presence as the source and sustainer of all of life. In the way in which this experience is conditioned by Christian faith, this feeling of absolute dependence is an experience of God as just, wise, dependable, and so forth, but most of all as love, for in the experience of having been redeemed we recognize that love is that most basic attribute of God which motivates God's self-imparting in creating and redeeming.

It is this experience of God as utterly dependable love which is the basis in

Schleiermacher's theology for the affirmation that God's absolute causality is the foundation of the whole natural order (ibid., 200, 211). This omnipotence of God is eternal and omnipresent. This means that in contrast to the Deistic view of a God who created the cosmos and then left it to run on its own, God's causality is always and everywhere at work. It includes finite causalities and transcends them. In contrast to the supernaturalistic view that divine power is more directly present in events that we cannot explain in terms of natural law, Schleiermacher judged that such a notion reduces God's eternal and omnipresent causality which is expressed in the natural order to a temporal, spatial, and inconsistent activity. "Rather everything is and becomes altogether by means of the natural order, so that each takes place through all and all wholly through the divine omnipotence, so that all indivisibly exists through One" (ibid., 212).

This interpretation of God's power seems at first to declare that that power is limited, for it says that God *cannot* intervene causally supplementing or displacing natural laws. But in Schleiermacher's judgment the idea of God intervening in such ways—or even being *able* to do so—is not an idea of greater power, but of less, for it presupposes God's inability to have created appropriately to the divine will.

Schleiermacher also rejected the idea that in creating God chose this creation from among various possibilities. Such a view assumes possibility to exist outside of God, whereas God is the source of both possibility and actuality, and the distinction does not apply to God. God is not a temporal being which can at one time consider various possibilities and at another actualize one or more of them. God is eternal and omnipresent, and ". . . the one all-embracing divine will is identical with the eternal omnipotence" (ibid., 218). Hence God's self-willing is as Creator and Sustainer, and the willing of the world is included therein (ibid., 217).

Since, as we must express it, this means that God did not have "options" about whether to create or what to create, this sounds like a denial of freedom or independence in God. Schleiermacher's position was that God is independent on his view, for ". . . there is nothing in God for which a determining cause is to be posited outside God" (ibid., 219). It is only the anthropomorphism that thinks of God as another finite being for which this seems to be a lack of freedom. But the freedom of even a greatest limited being is not, in Schleiermacher's judgment, what Christian faith experiences. Such a finite being cannot be absolutely dependable.

It is important to note here that Schleiermacher's conclusions are not the result of some blind acceptance of modern science. He did, indeed, accept the scientific experience of nature as orderly, but the basic reason for his interpretation of the reality and activity of God is the Christian experience of God's living presence as utterly dependable love. His understanding of that experience is influenced by Scripture and tradition as well as by science and piety.

Thus one returns to the question regarding the understanding of the decisiveness of Jesus Christ. Throughout its history Christianity has been characterized by the conviction that God acted decisively in Jesus to bring about the salvation or deliverance or redemption of humankind. (These three terms are but representative of many interpretive models or metaphors that Scripture and tradition have employed.) This has ordinarily been seen as an inbreaking from beyond. We can speak of this as a "supernatural causal intervention," provided we recognize that the meaning of this phrase is different in the era of modern science than it could have been in earlier times.

Schleiermacher insisted upon all of this, except he wished to avoid any affirmation of a disruption of the natural order. The apparently easy way to do this would be to interpret Jesus Christ as a development in human history of someone whose natural gifts made possible the decision to be wholly trusting in God and thus so open to grace as to be motivated only by a perfect God-consciousness. But Schleiermacher agreed with most of the Christian theological tradition that this would seriously underestimate the power of sin and make salvation a human achievement. For Schleiermacher the specific basis for rejecting such a view was that Christian religious experience is rooted in having been redeemed from sin by grace, not simply an experience of having been shown a better way that we were always capable of following.

The problem which Christian experience knows the Redeemer to have overcome is that human beings who were created originally capable of perfect God-consciousness have instead been dominated by sense-consciousness. This sinfulness may also be characterized as a turning away from God which is manifest in preoccupation with one's self and other finite realities. The power of the spirit is impeded by sensuousness. It began in a time when the God-consciousness had not yet actively emerged (ibid., 272–73), and Schleiermacher affirmed that it could be said to have been ordained by God insofar as it is entailed in the divine will to redeem humankind (ibid., 269). We do not have knowledge of just how the original turning away from God came about, but Christian experience does include the recognition that we are incapable of perfect God-consciousness, and only redemption can remove this incapacity (ibid., 282–83).

Christ's saving work, Schleiermacher taught, was made possible by a perfect God-consciousness which was his sole motivation (ibid., 415), and it is effected by his drawing others into the power of his God-consciousness (ibid., 425). The question this raises here is how—without supernatural causal intervention—Jesus could have had this perfect God-consciousness.

Schleiermacher's argument seems to be built upon at least two key affirmations. First, because human nature was originally such as to be capable of perfect God-consciousness, Jesus' having such did not make him essentially different from other human beings. He was actually different in that his life was not conditioned by descent and society like all others, and therefore he did not participate in the sinfulness of alienation from God which inevitably characterizes the lives of all others. Thus Jesus differed from all others, but he was truly human. That Jesus could thus be free from sin must be seen as a new creative act by God. This is where the second point of Schleiermacher's argument enters in, for he held that this act of God in completing the creation of humankind is not a disruption of the natural order. God's creative activity in itself transcends time. What to us may appear to be a disruptive incursion really is not, because it is encompassed in the one eternal creative decree (ibid., 365, 389).

Opinions differ as to whether Schleiermacher succeeded here in affirming that redemption is a gift of grace while yet avoiding any appeal to supernatural causal intervention. Both "liberal" and "conservative" critics have judged the answer to be no. From the more traditional standpoints it may be argued that Schleiermacher's effort and failure here demonstrate that Christian faith *cannot* be interpreted without acknowledging some supernatural causal intervention. More liberal critics may judge that Schleiermacher's failure here resulted rather from his unnecessary inference (from Christian experience) that human redemption could only come about by way of a special divine act through a person freed from the otherwise universal effects of human descent and society. Schleiermacher was being quite traditional in this, sharing the conviction that a human being can only become whole in conscious acceptance of Jesus as the Christ. This christocentric exclusivism is entangled with supernatural causal intervention, and it probably cannot be maintained without it.

Schleiermacher's theology was much criticized but also enormously influential throughout the nineteenth and into the twentieth century. It is not our concern here to pursue these issues, but only to introduce one of the ways in which modern liberal Christian theologians have sought to show that Christian faith is not incompatible with the world being described by science. Schleiermacher's way was to insist that religion is not to be understood primarily as a matter of knowing or of doing, but of the feeling of absolute dependence. On this basis he sought to show that God is not properly understood in the anthropomorphisms that implicitly finitize the Deity as a reality alongside the world occasionally intervening in its regularities. Rather, God is truly transcendent, different in kind, and therefore everywhere present as experienced in profound religious awareness. God's infinity encompasses the finite and is present in the finite. Thus, God is an active presence, experienced by faith, but this divine presence and activity do not displace the very laws of nature that express the divine creative will.

PAUL TILLICH: GOD AS ECSTATICALLY
KNOWN SPIRITUAL PRESENCE

Schleiermacher's general theological perspective has hardly been the only way of reinterpreting the activity of God in the world in modern theology, or even the dominant one. There are similarities, however, in some modern theologies, most notably that of Paul Tillich (1886–1965). He shared the basic judgment that faith's experience of the divine Spiritual Presence shows that God is not *a* being, thus in some sense a member of a class and subject to its structures. God is rather to be thought of as Being-itself, as the Ground and Power of Being.

Instead of "the feeling of absolute dependence," Tillich interpreted basic human experience in terms of "ultimate concern." On its negative side, this phrase points to the inevitable result of human self-consciousness, existential anxiety. That is, because we are quite consciously aware of ourselves, know that we can and will suffer pain, loneliness, guilt, and death, and struggle with the question as to whether our lives have any meaning, we are threatened in our very being. But this phrase, "ultimate concern," also has a positive use, for correlated with its employment to describe our utter threatenedness, Tillich also used it as a general description of faith, when that which is truly ultimate is what determines our being or not being. For the most part we seek our basic security in conditioned realities such as doctrines, rituals, wealth, possessions, power, self-righteousness, the praise of our neighbors, and so forth. This is idolatry, and it is self-defeating. Even when we do not realize it, it leaves us in the grip of existential anxiety which possesses and/or drives our lives. If, however, that which is ultimate is the "object" of our ultimate concern, is that which determines our being or not being, we are effectively (not totally) freed from such possession and drivenness.

Although Tillich's theology is profoundly influenced by the discoveries of the depth psychologists (which was not possible for Schleiermacher, whose work preceded that of Freud), Tillich's conviction about religion as ultimate concern meant that he shared Schleiermacher's judgment that religion is not primarily a matter of knowing or doing, but is a larger reality encompassing these dimensions of life. The intellectual exercise of believing in God—even with doctrines which very carefully deny all conditionedness of God and affirm true ultimacy—is in itself an act of less than the whole person. Thinking alone is not ultimate concern, and the same may be said of willing and doing. One of the more obvious reasons why so many "nonreligious" persons judge the religious to be hypocritical is that they can see that the doctrinal professions and the actual living of the "believers" are usually disparate. But in Tillich's judgment, those "nonreligious" persons are also self-deceived. They too, inevitably, are ultimately concerned, threatened in their very being, and desperately seeking some basis on which to accept and affirm themselves or to hide from their own existential anxieties. Usually, they, too, are idolators, even if less "hypocritical."

Faith, then, is not merely or primarily "belief." It is a state of being grasped by God, the Spiritual Presence, Holy and Gracious Being. God is a living and active presence that can be experienced, but not as a subject experiences an object. That in which we can find the adequate response to our ultimate concern is no finite and conditioned reality such that we can possess it, control it, or even define it. Tillich insisted that religious experience is "ecstatic." He did not mean by this a state of emotional frenzy and irrationality. Rather, he pointed to the roots of the term "ecstasy" as meaning "standing outside one's self," and interpreted this as indicating a state which transcends subject/object relatedness (Tillich 1951, 111–12). "Revelation" is one of the terms for this ecstatic experience of the divine presence about which more will be said in the next chapter. It is a way of affirming that God is active in human lives *without* accepting the idea of supernatural causal intervention. Tillich was explicit in his judgment that such supernaturalism finitizes God to the status of a being incapable of bearing the weight of ultimate concern. For Holy Being itself to interrupt or disrupt the structures of the creation would be for God to be in self-conflict, that is, to not be God.

These general conclusions about how God acts and the understanding of the God-world relationship on which they are based are very similar to Schleiermacher's. The meaning of this for the interpretation of the person and work of Jesus Christ is, however, different. The christocentric exclusivism, the view that only those who explicitly accept Jesus as the Christ can be "saved," is not only dropped, it is emphatically repudiated as incompatible with the sovereignty of grace that faith knows and proclaims. That Jesus could be received as the Christ is accounted for without appeal even to Schleiermacher's "relatively supernatural" explanation, in spite of the fact that human sinfulness is judged by Tillich to be a more serious matter than it was in Schleiermacher's theology.

One of the major cultural developments that took place during the century which separated the work of Schleiermacher from that of Tillich was the success of the evolutionary understanding of life and the cosmos. This provides a significantly altered context for understanding the origin of human sinfulness. Modern theologians have judged that the effort to base an explanation of the alienation between God and humankind on a literal interpretation of Genesis 3 is hopelessly fraught with contradiction. Schleiermacher argued this at some length, and concluded that since we have no access to the situation of "the first human pair," we can have no explanation of the fact of sin in creatures created capable of perfect God-consciousness. There are influential theologies today which share this judgment in one form or another, affirming that sin, the supposed choice of alienation from God, is utterly irrational and any effort to explain it is therefore a profound mistake.

Yet, if the origin of humankind in the evolutionary process is taken seriously, this whole problem may be seen very differently. The several sciences which study the development of the human species have found that Homo sapiens, humans as thinking beings, emerged only gradually over a very long period of time. Consciousness is understood to have developed slowly in our animal ancestors, and self-consciousness very slowly out of that prereflective consciousness. This development of consciousness and then self-consciousness, the latter being the distinguishing and enabling precondition of much of what we call "human," must have been an ever-increasing awareness of the threatenedness of these limited creatures. The emergence of self-consciousness, with its possibilities of reasoning, cooperating, communicating, toolmaking, and so on, inevitably entailed anxiety, the experience of being threatened in one's very being. That is to say, there is nothing whatsoever surprising or mysterious in the fact that humankind came into being with a basic motivation of anxious self-protectiveness. There was no literal Garden of Eden in our past, though we can see that our animal ancestors would have been much more "at home" in nature than their self-reflective descendants—including ourselves. Where "sin" is understood as a descriptive term for the absence of faith (the obvious proof text here is Paul's "whatever does not proceed from faith is sin" [Rom. 14:23]), or alienation from God, it is easily understood why the species and each individual within it have found themselves to be "sinful." There is no mystery in the fact that we are so anxious and so self-centered. Nor is it to be blamed on the body, for it is essentially a "spiritual" matter, accounted for in terms of the higher faculties, rather than the lower. Further, although it may be judged that the experience of guilt is a universal aspect of the processes of growth in humanness, on these grounds "sin" is not understood legalistically and juridically (on the models of the willful violation of law, etc.). In theologies like that of Tillich, the extensive treatment of these questions is informed not only by the acknowledgment of evolution but also by the insights of depth psychology. (See chaps. 3 and 4 of *Understanding Modern Theology I*.)

The human problem ("sin") and the divine solution ("salvation") must be understood in relation to each other in any coherent theology. The fact that this brief sketch concerning sin is placed here before any discussion of Tillich's understanding of the saving work of Jesus Christ does not mean that he determined the nature of human sinfulness first and then "tailored" the understanding of the person and work of Christ to fit. He was accused of this, because he treated the two subjects in this sequence. In his "method of correlation," he examines the human situation under the impact of the teachings of the church, and he examines these teachings of the church (the "theological answers") under the impact of the ways in which we may discern our being to be most deeply threatened in our historical-cultural context ("the existential questions"). This results in both factors being reformulated. A Christian theologian can only "see" our world in the light of the influence of the teachings of the Christian community which have brought him or her into the community of faith, and can only "hear" that proclamation in light of the ways in which he or she is experiencing that world. It is because of having experienced the new life in faith in response to the church's witness that the theologian knows Jesus to be the Christ and recognizes the human predicament to be, at its root, alienation from God.

From this point of view, then, the theologians know that Jesus is the "Christ" and that the witness of the church has enabled the taking of the risk of faith in which persons have been reconciled to God, to themselves, and to their neighbors. But they do *not* know that the particularities of the theological interpretations which have helped to keep that effective witness alive in other historical-cultural contexts are to be regarded as binding. Quite the contrary, in Tillich's judgment, today's theologians can see that the supernaturalism of premodern times which was inevitable for their interpretations and helpful to their proclamation is now a "false stumbling block," an impediment rather than a help in the affirmation of what God has done in Jesus Christ, for now it conveys the message that Christian faith is incompatible with the world as we experience it, and that God, rather than sovereign grace, had to act in self-contradiction to correct a flaw in creation. The proclamation of Jesus as the Christ *must not* be on the basis of supernatural causal intervention!

The Christologies based upon such divine intervention and which thereby describe a Jesus Christ who is essentially unlike all other human beings, having been exempted from even the possibility of alienation from God ("sin") and therefore from the most significant struggles and threats of human life, are judged unsound by Tillich. Indeed, it is precisely because the disciples experienced Jesus as essentially like themselves and subject to the same threats and temptations that they could be challenged by him, by his love, his freedom from anxiety, his denial of himself on behalf of his neighbors, to take the risk of letting go of their own anxious self-protectiveness, accepting the affirmation that they were accepted—in spite of their unacceptability—by the grace of God, a grace that they found embodied in Jesus.

It is the grace of God which is the source of salvation. Jesus was dependent on it, open to it, filled by it, and therefore he became "transparent" to it. Tillich's was a "relational" understanding of human being. Persons are not islands constituted simply by what they are in themselves. We are the specific persons which we are in large measure because of basic personal relationships that enter into our constitution. The depth psychologists in particular have developed the profound importance of such relationships for every person, but various philosophies, psychologies, theologies, and so on, have argued the same. These theologies have contended, however, that it is not just the conscious and unconscious relationships to parents, siblings, spouses, and so forth, which so profoundly make us what we are, for in their view, there is a more basic relationship—the relationship to God. Only God's love is unconditioned, freely given, and utterly trustworthy. Jesus' being was most deeply constituted by his openness to the graciousness of God, so "in Christ God was reconciling the world to himself" (2 Cor. 5:19), and John could interpret Jesus as saying, "I and the Father are one" (John 10:30). These texts have usually been interpreted as witnessing to Jesus' divinity, in keeping with the traditional supernaturalism, but which of these interpretations is more appropriate (if either) is subject to debate. It was Tillich's judgment that there is ample biblical evidence that Jesus was not proclaiming himself, that, indeed, he could be transparent to God because he did not point to himself but denied himself on behalf of his mission.

The question that must be asked here, then, is how Jesus could have become so profoundly open to the Spiritual Presence if this was not due to some divine causal intervention. It is due, of course, to "the acts of God," to the grace of God in creation, in history, in Jesus' life, but in Tillich's judgment this did not, could not, involve any violation of the utter dependability of God expressed, among other places, in what we call the laws of nature. Jesus' openness to God such that he could embody the reality of God for us and the fullness of humanity as intended by God must be understood as made *possible* by Jesus' heredity, family, culture, religion, freedom, and all the other factors which constitute a person's historical particularity and possibilities. God is at work within and around every person in every time, but the work of grace is not coercive (that would hardly be "grace").

Does this mean, speaking theoretically, that someone else might have been the Christ? "Speaking theoretically," yes, said Tillich. But no one else was received as the Christ, and whether in actuality someone else might have been the coming together of the myriad factors making possible both such a risk and vocation and such a historical-cultural setting as to be recognized as the bearer of the reality and the will of God is utterly speculative. What Christian faith knows is that the community of faith in which we participate came into being in response to Jesus.

On such a basis, Tillich repudiated christocentric exclusivism. The God whom we have come to know through the faith which we have risked in response to the church's witness to Jesus as the Christ is the Spiritual Presence active everywhere and always. Every genuine religion is a response to that gracious Presence. For Christians considering non-Christian religions this is most obviously true for Judaism, for the history and witness of that community were a crucial dimension of Jesus' own life and possibilities. But the affirmation of religions is not limited to this forebear of Christianity. This did not mean, for Tillich, that all religions are equal. There are profound differences among them. For Christians, Jesus Christ is the norm by which they judge the degree to which the Spiritual Presence has been appropriately responded to—not only in other religions, but in Christianity as well. Tillich's theology is Spirit-centered and Christo-normative.

Tillich's theology, then, is one in which an effort has been carried out to interpret Christian faith entirely without recourse to supernatural causal intervention, for he judged that any such appeal implicitly denies that divine grace is sovereign. It is not a theology in which God is understood to be either absent, inactive, or ineffective. As with Schleiermacher, God is understood to be a living presence, infinite being which encompasses finite being, the source and sustainer of all that is, acting in and upon every person, Spirit with spirit, in a way which is consistent with the purposes of grace, and therefore with the freedom and responsibility of spiritual beings. The two theologies are also different in many ways, for Tillich, writing roughly a century later than Schleiermacher, shared the general judgment of the theologians of the twentieth century that Schleiermacher had underestimated the depth and seriousness of human sinfulness and failed to see that it is essentially a matter of spirit. Further, influenced by many developments in the natural and social sciences and in biblical scholarship, Tillich carried the implications of this type of reinterpretation further than Schleiermacher and avoided the inconsistency regarding the Christ-event.

This approach which insisted—on the basis of Christian religious experience—that God is more transcendent than a being beside other beings, a reality beside the cosmos who must intervene in its divinely given regularities from time to time in order to attain the divine purposes, and is a mysterious but experienceable presence, more immanent and active than the traditional supernaturalism conceives, is hardly the only type of reinterpretation of how God acts in modern theology. Indeed, the views of both Schleiermacher and Tillich have received far more criticism than approval even from "liberal" theologians. The frequency with which both have been charged with "mysticism" and "pantheism" is indicative of the most common type of disagreement, in spite of the fact that the charge of pantheism can only be characterized as silly. They were both clear in affirming the transcendence as well as the immanence of God and insisting upon the difference of God from the whole creation within which God is, nevertheless, present. The applicability of the charge of "mysticism" depends upon the definition of the term, for they were, indeed, affirming a "mystical presence" of God "knowable" in a kind of experience that transcends subject/object relationships.

GORDON KAUFMAN: THE HISTORY OF
THE COSMOS AS GOD'S
MASTER ACT

An example of a different kind of modern theological answer to these questions is found in the work of Harvard University theologian Gordon Kaufman (b. 1925). He shares the judgment that Christian theology must be profoundly reinterpreted in view of the vast changes in our experience and understanding of the world and that this must include reinterpretation of the understanding of the way in which God acts in and upon creation. Yet the difference from views like those of Schleiermacher and Tillich is clearly to be seen precisely in the understanding of this issue concerning "how God acts."

Kaufman rejects the idea that there is any such thing as the "religious experience" which is so basic to the theologies of Schleiermacher and Tillich and their teachings concerning God's activity among us (Kaufman 1968a, 200; 1975, 5; 1981, 70). In some of his writings it would also appear that Kaufman disagrees with the conception of God as infinite Being encompassing finite being or as Ground and Power of Being rather than *a* being, the perspective which underlies Schleiermacher's and Tillich's interpretations of "the acts of God." Kaufman has held that "God" is a proper name for a personal being, an active independent agent, dependent upon the creation in *no* respect, and free to reveal or not reveal himself to human beings (Kaufman 1968b, 168; 1971, 99). Yet this has been accompanied by insistence that God is beyond our human powers to conceive and should not be thought of as like other beings. In more recent writings his expressions sound less like the earlier and more traditional formulations of a divine being which breaks into history from beyond (Kaufman 1968b, 377) and more like Tillich's conception. In *The Theological Imagination: Constructing the Concept of God,* for example, Kaufman says, ". . . God symbolizes that in the ongoing evolutionary-historical process which grounds our being as distinctively human and which draws (or drives) us on toward authentic human fulfillment (salvation)" (Kaufman 1981, 41). He adds here that "God continues to symbolize that which is outside and other than the human . . ." (ibid.) and notes that he is no longer convinced of the necessity of affirming ". . . belief in God's existing over against us . . . " (ibid., 37) so there is no longer a clear contrast with the views of Schleiermacher and Tillich on this point. All three affirm the transcendence as well as the immanence of God and criticize finitizing concepts of God as idolatrous. They clearly differ, nevertheless, concerning God's acts and the mode of God's presence, and when Kaufman addressed this question most directly in 1968 he judged his own position to represent a concept of God which differed substantially from Tillich's. Kaufman's contention was that God can and should be regarded as an *Agent,* one who acts, whose purposes and intentions are realized in and through creation (Kaufman 1968a, 180).

Kaufman was not defending the traditional assumption of a causally intervening activity of God, for he argued that modern experience (including science) is not compatible with such a view (ibid., 184–89). But he also judged that it is a misleading use of language to speak of "acts of God" when we intend to refer only to an "immanent teleology," that is, to some "goal" or directedness internal to nature or the cosmos (ibid., 181). An "act" involves the intentions and purposes of an agent who thus adds an element of creativity to the situation. Thus taking "human purposive behavior" as the model, Kaufman defined an "act of God" as "a deed performed by God, i.e., an event which did not simply 'happen,' but which was what it was because God did it" (ibid., 183).

The way in which Kaufman was able to affirm such "acts of God" without falling back into the unacceptable notion of miraculous interventions was by arguing that this phrase, "act of God," should be used primarily to refer to God's "master act" which is *"the whole course of history,* from its initiation in God's creative activity to its consummation when God ultimately achieves his purposes" (ibid., 191). It is this ongoing act of God that provides the order of nature which modern science depends upon and within which more particular events such as the development of the solar system, the emergence of life on earth, or the exodus may be seen as "sub-acts." This means that besides those events emphasized in the biblical narratives, events in the histories of other cultures and more recent events in the Western world may also "be seen as governed or guided by the activity through which God is moving the whole creation toward the eschaton . . ." (ibid., 198).

Kaufman did not mean to suggest that every happening is to be regarded as a sub-act of God's master act, but only those events which facilitate the fulfillment of God's ultimate intentions for the creation (ibid.). These events can only be distinguished because God, the cosmic agent, has chosen to reveal the divine purposes (ibid., 194).

This appeal to revelation sounds at first like a contradiction of the interpretation of God's acts which Kaufman was proposing, but "revelation" is itself being reinterpreted. Kaufman's position suggests that God's self-disclosure is *through* developing cultural traditions rather than by incursions into them, for the latter would violate the freedom and cultural creativity that are among the essential human characteristics which faith discerns as expressive of the divine intentions (Kaufman 1972, 164). Here again, Kaufman appeals to the analogy of human relations. He points out that persons are known ("revealed") to one another through the sharing of a common language and history (ibid., 156) rather than through objective information and immediate encounters. With God we neither have direct encounters nor share a common language, but analogously to the sharing of a common history with other persons, God may be seen to be revealed through history, the history in which we live and which is the ongoing master act of God. The long development of human life and of historical-cultural settings was necessary for the possibility of receiving such revelation, and in the evolution of religion, "God was beginning to accomplish his intention of revealing himself to man" (ibid., 162). Thus the same developments that can be interpreted as natural or accidental can also be judged to manifest a deeper guiding purpose, the purpose of God.

This sounds like a "natural theology," but that was not Kaufman's intention. As he put it in another article, "If God, then, is the name of an individual agent—indeed, of *the individual* to which no other is properly comparable—then knowledge of him, if any is to be had by men, will have to be gained through our concrete historical relations with him. God will be known in and through a positive history, not primarily through general ideas, theoretical constructs, or extrapolations from and interpretations of common experience" (Kaufman 1971, 100). In later writings Kaufman has sought to make the point in less traditional language. He argues that it is no longer reasonable to ground theology on direct appeals to the authority of revelation, because it is first necessary to develop a concept of God which any appeal to revelation presupposes. Nevertheless, he affirms that the view that revelation is "the ultimate ground of theological knowledge is not . . . entirely misguided" when it is understood "that it is precisely through the constructive work of the human imagination that God—ultimate reality understood as active and beneficent, as 'gracious'—makes himself known" (Kaufman 1975, 64). Here again one can see an illustration of the point that when the understanding of God's activity as supernatural causal intervention is rejected, the old distinction of "natural theology" and "revealed theology" is no longer meaningful. From a supernaturalistic standpoint, Kaufman's proposal will be seen as "natural theology," but this only means that such a viewpoint continues to assume the traditional understanding of "acts of God" which Kaufman judges to be incoherent in the modern world. On his own view, theology is "imaginative construction" responding to the self-revealing activity of God in and through the processes of nature and history.

In this way, then, Kaufman is able to deny supernatural causal intervention and yet affirm that God acts in the world in an absolutely essential way. At the same time, the appeal to revelation as the basis for discerning which events are God's sub-acts helping to fulfill the divine intentions seems to be part of a circular—and therefore unsatisfactory—argument. The history itself, insofar as it moves toward God's full purposes, *is* the revelation that is supposed to enable us to judge which events are God's sub-acts which reveal God's purposes. That is, the same events which we need to judge by the aid of revelation constitute that revelation!

A fuller account is offered by Kaufman in his more recent book, *The Theological Imagination*. Here he has developed the thesis that theology is—and always has been—*imaginative construction*. He is certainly not suggesting that theologians "dream up" depictions of God and human destiny. He is, rather, making the following points: (1) God is never an object of human perception available for observation and description. (2) God transcends all human conceptions. (3) Historical scholarship has shown that biblical and creedal formulations are historically and culturally relative human interpretations and not miraculously given "truths." (4) Therefore, every theological teaching has been and must be a human attempt to offer a helpful imaginative construction of that which is the ultimate center of devotion and orientation for persons of monotheistic belief. (5) Since many forms of modern learning have together made the foregoing points both clear and inescapable, theology can today be consciously and self-critically aware of its constructive character as never before (Kaufman 1981, 29–32). The work of theology is necessarily an activity carried on under the impact of a community of faith because only the influence of such traditions could provide the possibility and the impetus for such constructive efforts. Theology is thus a response to "revelation" as Kaufman has redefined that concept (ibid., 31).

Kaufman argues that there are three principal criteria for this responsive-imaginative "constructing toward God." He designates these "absoluteness," "humaneness," and "presence" (ibid., 267–72). "The Principle of God's Absoluteness" points to the judgment that God is the ultimate point of reference and unlimited devotion. To give oneself to anything less than the ultimate, to conceive of God as limited, finite, or even properly conceivable by finite minds, is to fall into idolatry and suffer destructive consequences (ibid., 268–69). Accordingly, any image or concept employed in our efforts to express the reality intended by the symbol "God" must be seen as no more than a model, metaphor, or analogy. "The Principle of God's Humaneness" emphasizes the primacy in Christian tradition of human models and metaphors for conceiving God and affirming divine concern for human development and fulfillment. Jesus Christ as primary Christian criterion means that God must be understood essentially as suffering and forgiving love, thus, as *humane* (ibid., 270–71). Taken together, these two criteria require the rejection of any claims of absoluteness (for anything other than God, including our doctrines of God) and any inhumane or dehumanizing activities or structures, whether these be in theology, church, politics, society, or anywhere else. To proclaim the absoluteness of the humane God is to enhance human growth

and fulfillment, but to claim absolute status for any of our doctrines (or structures) is to commit idolatry and contribute to the destruction of human life.

To these two theological criteria of absoluteness and humaneness Kaufman
adds a third which he calls "presence." He is not suggesting now that there is
the sort of "religious experience" of God which we have seen in Schleiermacher and in Tillich. Rather, he is affirming that one of the essential tasks of
theology is so to express the absoluteness and humaneness of God as to make
clear God's meaningfulness and relevance in each contemporary situation.
Hence "imaginative construction" must be the continuing character of theology. In the absence of ongoing theological reconstruction, meaning is lost,
idolatry develops, and dehumanization results (ibid., 272–76).

These three formal criteria as given material content in Christian theology
by Jesus Christ as norm provide the basis for discerning which events are to
be seen as God's acts ("sub-acts" in the earlier terminology), including revelation. More specifically, they enable the discernment of God's activity seen
as the thrust toward humanization in the whole historical process (ibid., 38,
144). It can also be readily seen that other religious traditions will not be
judged to be false and destructive simply because they do not accept Jesus as
the Christ, but will be judged by Christians in accordance with these same
criteria—with the expectation that this thrust toward humanization (God's
self-revealing activity) will to some extent be manifest there also.

Clearly Kaufman differs considerably from the more traditional and orthodox Christologies. In his judgment the historical reality of Jesus was over-
whelmed by mythic interpretation in much of the history of Christian
theology. Though this is understandable within previous world views, we can
now see how the supernaturalistic depictions of Jesus Christ as the "mighty
Lord of history" contributed to much self-aggrandizement, cruelty, and war-
fare in Christian history (ibid., 140–41).

The human problem for which Christianity has seen the solution in Jesus
Christ is that as finite self-conscious beings we are motivated to seek security
and satisfaction. Individually we put ourselves at the center of our worlds, we
identify with our groups over against others, and we put human needs and
desires above all other concerns. Something is needed, therefore, to break
into this self-centeredness, enabling persons to place their devotion in a legitimate center of meaning beyond themselves (ibid., 36).

. The Christian conviction is that this happened in Jesus Christ. History had
its critical turning point in his life, death, and resurrection, and the Christian
community participates—albeit very ambiguously—in an ongoing historical
process of reconciliation enabled by the acceptance of the crucified Jesus as
the key to understanding the character of ultimate reality as suffering love
(Kaufman 1968b, 404ff).

In his *Systematic Theology: A Historicist Perspective* (1968), Kaufman insisted that the Christ-event *began* this historical process. He argued that once humankind had chosen to make themselves the center of their lives, they became captive to this sinfulness, and any solution had to be a breaking into history in a decisive act by God (ibid., 413, 428–29). Clearly this language invites supernaturalistic interpretation, even though the book as a whole resists it. Among the many places where this is clear is the discussion of the resurrection. Kaufman took the view that the community's conviction that God had decisively broken into history in Jesus (whom they could therefore see as the embodiment of both humanity and divinity) came about—and probably could only have come about—because of their belief that they had encountered the resurrected Jesus. But he also argued that we cannot share their interpretations today, and the real issue is not whether the individual person Jesus was alive again, but whether a new community of love was realizing God's purposes in history. What the disciples understood as appearances of their risen Lord had and has its import in their trust in the continuing presence of God's redeeming love (ibid., 411–34). This discussion of the resurrection is too complex to be summarized adequately here. Its importance in this context is its indication of Kaufman's desire to avoid a supernaturalist interpretation of Christianity even in his affirmation of a decisive breaking into history in God's redeeming act.

In a more recent book, *The Theological Imagination* (1981), Kaufman no longer talks of "God's act breaking into history." Indeed, such language seems to be in severe tension with the view of God's "master act" set forth in the essay of 1968. In its terms the divine "sub-act" of the incarnation could be seen as a decisive manifestation of God's "master act" constituting the whole historical process, but hardly as a "breaking in." Here God is described as the reality which is expressed in the whole cosmic process of evolution and history which is moving humanity toward its authentic fulfillment (Kaufman 1981, 150).

How could the quite-human Jesus have become the person who could have evoked this faith and community, one whose life could be seen as both the realization of authentic human existence and the embodiment of the character of ultimate reality? Since supernatural causal intervention is ruled out, one infers that Jesus' heredity, history, community, family, and responsible decisions in response to the divine thrust toward humanity, which had already been affirmed—even if ambiguously—in Jesus' history and community, are the kinds of factors which Kaufman would point to in response to this question, noting that we cannot have a definite answer.

This interpretation of the Christ-event without appeal to divine causal intervention (yet with the insistence that God is the primary and ultimate factor at work) sounds very much like the teaching of Tillich described above. Important differences should not be overlooked, however. Although both theologians have judged that the traditional appeals to miraculous interventions disrupting nature are incompatible with our experience of reality, and both affirm that God is the guiding impetus of the whole cosmic history, they nevertheless also differ in their understandings of the way in which God and humans are related. Tillich affirmed that God is an active living presence which can be "ecstatically" experienced by persons. Faith is not just or even primarily an intellectual commitment, but a relationship involving every dimension of self.

Kaufman repudiates such claims of religious experience as meaningless. Accordingly God's presence and activity are something to be *believed in.* From his point of view Tillich's affirmation of religious experience and understanding of faith manifest the errors of "mysticism." From Tillich's point of view Kaufman's understandings of God, humanity, and faith represent the distortions of rationalism.

Kaufman's viewpoint is "rationalistic," however, in a particular Kantian sense. The suggestion is certainly not that he is a "metaphysical" rationalist, that is, one who holds that reality has the basic characteristics of human reason. Nor is it that Kaufman is an "epistemological" rationalist, one who holds that reason rather than sense experience is the principal source of knowledge. Indeed, Kaufman may be more Kantian than any other well-known theologian today. Kant's work marks a major watershed in the history of philosophy precisely in his arguments against metaphysical and epistemological rationalisms. Kant contended that human knowledge is of *phenomena* only, never of *noumena* (the "real" in itself). That is, we know anything only as it is conditioned by the human capacities to have experience. Our basic categories for understanding are just that, *our* categories, "forms" of human understanding, characteristic equipment of the human mind. We must understand in terms of these forms, but that is no basis whatsoever for supposing that they apply to reality as it is in itself. Further, "concepts without percepts are empty." The categories and the concepts developed on their basis do not have any clear meaning for us except as they are given content by sense perceptions. Therefore, they *cannot* offer knowledge of the real in itself (the noumenal). Our sense perceptions are all conditioned by our particular capacities for receiving sense data, and these, in turn, are without meaning until they are organized by the minds of those having the experience and interpreted by the concepts. "Percepts without concepts are blind." (For an explanation of Kant's teaching, see *Understanding Modern Theology I*, chap. 2.)

As regards this critique of metaphysical and epistemological rationalisms, Schleiermacher, Tillich, and Kaufman are all "post-Kantian." They seek to build upon the basis of a general acknowledgment of Kant's work. Schleiermacher and Tillich argued that though Kant's arguments against metaphysical and epistemological rationalism were generally correct, Kant had misunderstood the nature of *religious* experience. Kant had no place for "the feeling of absolute dependence," "ultimate concern," or "ecstatic" experience of the Spiritual Presence. He sought a "religion within the limits of reason alone." It is reasoning which he saw as the essential human characteristic. He was a "rationalist," therefore, in his interpretation of human being and of what is meaningful for human beings. It is this "rationalism" which is to be seen in Kaufman from a viewpoint like Schleiermacher's or Tillich's. They affirm conscious reasoning as important, but not as *the* essential characteristic of human being. The difference is greater for Tillich, for he alone among the three is fundamentally influenced by depth psychology, including Jung's affirmation of the "collective unconscious." (See *Understanding Modern Theology I*, chap. 4.)

SCHUBERT OGDEN: GOD IN THE PROCESS

In contrast to these three "post-Kantian" viewpoints, there is a very influential modern theological perspective which in most of its representatives rejects Kant's critique of metaphysical and epistemological rationalism and therewith the contention (in Schleiermacher, Tillich, *and* Kaufman) that our doctrines can never be supposed to be correct descriptions of God. The several theologies being spoken of here are spoken of together as "process theology." I put it this way, because there is a considerable variety of theologies that build upon the "process philosophies" of Alfred North Whitehead, Charles Hartshorne, and their followers. Whereas Kant sought to show that the application of our concepts to God leads us inevitably into contradictions, the process philosophers propose the use of different concepts for understanding reality, including God. One of their arguments has been that modern science has shown that reality is not constituted basically by enduring substances as was supposed in the traditional metaphysics criticized by Kant. Rather, reality can now be seen to have the character of "energy" or "event" or "process." A whole new set of concepts is required for understanding reality as it is "seen" by the aid of modern science, and this offers a new conceptuality for the work of theology, a conceptuality which, its proponents believe, is not only more adequate to modern experience but also more adequate for interpreting the biblical witness. Among other things, this opens up possibilities for reinterpreting "how God acts."

One Christian theologian who has employed the concepts of process philosophy for reinterpreting God's activity is Schubert Ogden (b. 1928). Although Ogden is usually described as a "process theologian," it should be noted that his basic commitment is not to process philosophy but to Christian faith, as is evident in some departures in his teachings from some of the teachings of Whitehead and/or Hartshorne that are followed by various other "process theologians." (A helpful explication of differences among several prominent "process theologies"—including Ogden's—is provided by Robert Neville in his *Creativity and God: A Challenge to Process Theology*.) Ogden has frequently affirmed two general criteria for current Christian theological work, namely, appropriateness to the historic Christian witness (the "apostolic norm") and understandability "to human existence as judged in terms of common experience and reason" (Ogden 1979, 122). He believes that the *use* of process metaphysics will aid theology *both* to be loyal to the historic witness and to be understandable in our historical-cultural context.

Ogden calls the theology developed with the aid of the conceptuality of process philosophy "neoclassical theism," and specifies that its defining characteristic is the conception of God as "dipolar." By contrast, "classical theism" is understood to be "monopolar." In those traditional concepts God was held to be "simple," meaning that there was no joining together of constituents in God, for that would require, they judged, something "higher" which could provide a basis for the joining. But there can be nothing higher than God. God was therefore "pure being." This conception of the perfection of God was understood to mean that nothing could be added to God, and nothing could affect God from outside of God's own being, for there could be no contingency in God.

The conception of God as "dipolar" proposes a different understanding of "perfection." It proposes that God should be understood in terms of two basic factors. The abstract being of God, God's "primordial nature," is that which is unchanging, subject to no contingency. God has "aseity," does not derive being from something else and cannot be destroyed. But, it is argued, there is also God's "consequent nature." God is intimately related to all else and "knows" or "experiences" (the technical term in process thought is "prehends") all events. This means that God's consequent nature is continually changing. It is ever-growing, for God forgets nothing and is ever taking more into the divine "knowledge" and "memory." In contrast to the classical theistic conception of God as unchanging absolute (as the tradition is interpreted by process philosophers and theologians), this neoclassical theism views God as neither absolute nor relative, but as *both* absolute and relative, supremely absolute and supremely relative. God is as nothing else is or can be, and God cannot cease to be, but this absoluteness is an absolute relatedness, for God is intimately related to all.

Another way to put it is to say that neoclassical theism makes a distinction between God's *existence* and God's *actuality*. God's existence is absolute, but God's actuality, the particular state in which God actually is at any particular time, is thoroughly relative. God is thus depicted as "alive," not just static "being," but "becoming" along with all else. Such a God responds and can be judged therefore to be an appropriate object of worship to whom it makes sense to address prayer. Of course, worship and prayer have always been central to the life of the church. The point being made by the process theologians is that the traditional theistic conceptuality of the church's theologians was in severe tension with the religious life of the church. When God is understood as dipolar, related, alive, and becoming, this tension is removed, they believe.

God is thus described as in process and in the whole process which is reality. This means that God must be thought of as temporal, in some sense "in time." That judgment was repudiated by the more traditional theologies, for it was judged that in declaring God to be subject to such a structure as time (understood to be a structure of finitude, a limitation), it made God less than the structures of being, not the Creator from whom all else—including the structures of finite being—has received its being. This traditional denial of divine temporality has always posed some problems for believers. It was affirmed, for example, that what is future for us is "present" for God. God "knows the future" not because of "foreseeing" (which would be temporal), but because God transcends time, is "beyond" temporality. But, if the future, being present to God, is known to God, how can we suppose that our present has any genuine meaning or that we have any freedom of choice? Such questions are removed by the dipolar conception of God.

To the question as to whether God is then subject to the structures of being rather than being their source, the process thinkers, following Whitehead, have answered that God is not an exception to the metaphysical principles, but is rather their chief exemplification. On the one hand, this means that God is not understood as ultimate reality itself, is not identified with creativity itself, but is a being which is limited in various ways among which are the freedom and creativity of creatures. On the other hand, God is not a creature dependent for its existence upon some other actuality, but is that unique being "upon whose wisdom all forms of order depend" (Whitehead 1926, 328). Lewis Ford has argued that Whitehead's conception of God has several advantages over the more traditional views, including the affirmation of real freedom in the creatures whose actions are neither somehow also God's actions and are not foreknown by God, and the freeing of God from responsibility for evil by its removal of the traditional identification of God with all creativity (Ford 1970, 141). This is usually seen as a clear denial of the traditional Christian affirmation that God creates *ex nihilo* (from nothing) according to which God transcends the metaphysical structures of the cosmos of which God is the source in a divine freedom which is beyond human comprehension, and God is limited by nothing other than the divine nature and will. Ogden has argued that the neoclassical conception, while genuinely differing from the classical theistic view of God as Creator, nevertheless preserves the real motive of the doctrine of *creatio ex nihilo*, which is "to deny, against all forms of metaphysical dualism, that there is any being or principle save God alone which is the necessary ground of whatever exists or is even possible" (Ogden 1963, 62). He acknowledges that any particular state of the world had its potentiality "in the conjoint actuality of God and of the creatures constituting the precedent actual world (or worlds)" (ibid., 63). In the neoclassical view God is understood always to have existed together with *some* world, never in isolation, so there are always factors placing some limits upon the divine creativity, but no particular state of the world is itself necessary or eternal, as is God. God is thus understood to be essentially different from all creatures. Whether this view maintains what is essential in the tradition's affirmation of God as Creator is a matter of dispute among interpreters and critics of process theology.

One of the advantages of the neoclassical view that God is not an exception to the metaphysical principles—in the judgment of its proponents—is that it reduces the problem of knowing and understanding God. When God is understood as being a transcendent source of the principles, structures, and forms of any world and in no sense subject to or exemplifying them, it is difficult to see any basis for supposing that we creatures could have any genuine knowledge of God or speak correctly about God. This has been and continues to be a matter of serious study and dispute in theology, and various theological viewpoints have affirmed, indeed insisted, that we cannot have objective knowledge of God or speak of God correctly. In the neoclassical view, however, the affirmation that God is the *chief exemplification* of the metaphysical principles rather than an exception to them means that it is possible to understand and speak appropriately of God.

In 1963 Ogden approached this through what Whitehead called "the reformed subjectivist principle," "that the whole universe consists of elements disclosed in the analysis of the experiences of subjects . . . [and] apart from the experiences of subjects there is nothing . . ." (Whitehead 1929, 522–24). That of which we have the most direct knowledge is our own experiencing, yet the traditional attempts to deal with the problem of knowledge of God have assumed that anything real must be of the character of an *object* of our perception. From this assumption has developed the view that a being is a "substance" (Ogden 1963, 57). If instead we make that which we directly know, our "self," the model of the real, we begin on surer ground and with a very different conception.

The proposal which Ogden made is that "God must be conceived in strict analogy with ourselves." It must be *analogy*, for the concepts which apply to us apply to God "only in an eminent sense . . ." (ibid., 59). There is both genuine likeness and real difference between ourselves and God. God is to be conceived as both a temporal and a social being, such as we are, but God's uniqueness is maintained, for God is "the one reality which is eminently social and temporal." God is the perfect instance of creative becoming (ibid.). This qualitative difference of God from all else is not that God is to be conceived as utterly "bodiless," for God is rather to be understood as "the *eminently* incarnate One." The whole universe may be spoken of as God's "body," for God is immediately and directly in interaction with it. The universe is not external to God (ibid., 60).

This approach to the interpretation of the relationship of God and the universe is itself part of the understanding of "how God acts" in the world, and it is also the basis for further clarification. Just as God is to be understood in strict analogy with the self, God's action is to be understood by strict analogy with human actions. Ogden argues that the first thing which is meant by a human action is the "inner act whereby the human self as such is constituted, and constituted, moreover, as a self who loves" (ibid., 177).

> Behind all its public acts of word and deed there are the self's own private purposes or projects, which are themselves matters of action or decision. Indeed, it is only because the self first acts to constitute itself, to respond to its world, and to decide its own inner being that it "acts" at all in the more ordinary meaning of the word; all its outer acts of word and deed are but ways of expressing and implementing the inner decisions whereby it constitutes itself as a self. (Ibid.)

Most basic to this self-constituting act of a person is the choice between relating to the world by opening oneself in love and closing oneself in estrangement. All outward acts will be but reflections of this primary inner act.

On this basis Ogden proposes that the primary meaning of "act of God" is (analogously) that God is self-constituted as pure and unbounded love, committed to full participation in the world of creatures. It is therefore possible to understand this active relationship of God to the world as analogous to the relationship of the human mind to the human body. "The whole world is, as it were, his sense organ, and his interaction with every creature is unimaginably immediate and direct" (ibid., 178). Those for whom God is Redeemer understand that the destiny of human beings is, therefore, not only to contribute to their own and their world's self-creation, but is also to contribute to the self-creativity of God, "who accepts us without condition into his own everlasting life, where we have a final standing or security that can nevermore be lost" (ibid.).

Taking up the question of the meaning of the traditional Christian affirmation of acts of God in history, Ogden contends that God's actions should be understood as transcending history rather than as being *in* history, and God's actions should never be identified with particular historical events, not even God's acts as Redeemer (ibid., 179). God's activity is that in which God is ever actualizing his own essence by loving response to the creatures. To reduce this to particular acts in history would be to reduce God's eminent historicity to creaturely historicity, and that is self-contradictory.

On the analogy of the relationship of the human mind to the human body, it is possible to affirm that insofar as our bodily acts are expressive of our primary inner acts as selves, analogously, every creature is in some degree an act of God. Because human beings have understanding and can symbolize meaning, they have a special capacity to speak for or "re-present" the divine. In some cases it may be judged that the very activity of God is expressed by human action. "Any event, whether intended by anyone as symbolic or not, can become such an act of God insofar as it is received by someone as a symbol of God's creative and redeeming action" (ibid., 183). Thus, to say that God acts in history is to affirm that some particular human deeds and words have effectively re-presented God's characteristic activity, God's activity as Creator and Redeemer which is everywhere and always.

According to Ogden, Christians are persons whose constitutive understanding of themselves and of all existence is in response to the church's witness that in Jesus this active reality of God as sovereign love was decisively represented (ibid., 186). It is the conviction of Christian faith that Jesus was, therefore, God's act in history. This is an affirmation that for Christians Jesus is final revelation. Any tentative or partial affirmation of the revelation in Jesus Christ would not be "decisive" or "constitutive." It would not be faith. But this affirmation of "final revelation" is neither a denial of effective representations of the reality of God elsewhere nor an affirmation of a supernatural causal intervention. "The real meaning of the exclusiveness of Jesus Christ's lordship is not that divine lordship is exercised solely in that particular life, but rather that wherever such lordship is exercised—and that, naturally, is everywhere . . .—it can take no other form than the same promise and demand re-presented *for us* in Jesus" (ibid., 203).

In more recent writings, Ogden has made a shift in his position which affects the foregoing discussion. He has not, to be sure, altered his opposition to the notion of miraculous interventions, but he has concluded that the emphasis upon *analogy* in theology is misguided. In *The Point of Christology* he argues that a coherent metaphysical theism requires "strictly literal" affirmations regarding God (Ogden 1982, 140–47). The problem he now sees in his previous emphasis on analogy is that there is no satisfactory way of distinguishing the analogical from the "merely metaphorical or symbolic." On such a basis God may be "nothing more than the otherwise obscure 'whence' of my freedom and responsibility to love my fellow human beings . . ." (ibid., 132). This, in Ogden's judgment, leaves the credibility of Christian faith in serious doubt.

Ogden does not suggest that all of our theological and religious affirmations should be or could be literal. Quite the contrary. The statement that God is boundless love is, in his judgment, symbolic, for it uses reference to a human way of being in a secondary sense in order to speak of God (ibid., 144). Such an affirmation can escape the problem of vagueness only by having its place in a theology that makes literal metaphysical assertions as aspects of a fully worked out philosophical theology. ". . . Unless it is to be 'only a symbol' in the pejorative sense of being only apparently but not really true, the literal metaphysical assertions that alone suffice to make it true must assert all and not merely some of the conditions that are necessarily implied in making it" (ibid., 145). For example, in order for it to be true symbolically that God is boundless love, it must be literally true that God as ultimate reality is both individual and universal and that God acts upon and is acted upon by all things (ibid., 145). That is to say, Ogden's process metaphysics must be literally true if Christian faith is to maintain credibility.

Thus Ogden's theological perspective is very different from those sketched previously. In his view, none of those theologies offers a credible account of the acts of God, either in general or more specifically in Jesus Christ, because their analogical (Kaufman) or symbolic (Schleiermacher and Tillich) affirmations do not offer clarity or knowledge. For Ogden, human being is understood primarily in terms of conscious reason, and reality can be properly described in categories that are literally understood by human reason. In this last judgment the contrast with Kaufman is about the nature of reality. The contrast with Tillich is not only about the nature of reality but also in the understanding of human being and meaning.

At the risk of oversimplification, one might say that according to Ogden's theology, we can *know* that we are loved by God; according to Kaufman's theology, we can *believe* that we are loved by God; according to Tillich's theology, we can *experience* that we are loved by God. Such a comparison, however, should be seen as no more than suggestive of the different outlooks. Even the terms emphasized here are used differently in the three contexts. Ogden, for example, affirms that human beings have immediate experience of God (ibid., 138), but he does not mean thereby what Tillich means in describing "religious experience."

Thus far in this chapter four modern theological reinterpretations of the ways in which God is active in the world have been sketched. All four argue that the continuation of the common premodern assumption that the world suffers many and various supernatural incursions—including "acts of God" —must now be seen to deny not only our understanding of the world, but also the sovereignty of divine grace. In spite of the many important disagreements among these theologians, they all agree—in general—that God must be understood more as an inclusive and pervasive presence active within the whole creation than as a being acting upon it from outside, and the three twentieth-century interpreters judge that this enables us to see the error in the rejection of the other religions which is entailed in the traditional affirmation of divine interventions.

KARL BARTH: CHRISTIAN FAITH IS RESPONSE TO GOD'S SUPERNATURAL ACTS

Many modern theologians do not share the judgment that divine interventions should be denied, however. By "modern" here, I do not mean anyone who is now or has been recently a writer in the field of theology. Many such writers are hardly to be called "modern" in theology, for they oppose or show no awareness of the developments being described in this work. There are, however, theologians who recognize the realities of historical and cultural relativity and affirm the work of modern historical-critical biblical scholarship, but judge that Christian faith must be understood as involving supernatural causal interventions. Indeed, the man who is possibly the most influential of all twentieth-century theologians, Karl Barth (1886–1968), fought for this very judgment.

In Barth's opinion, theological viewpoints such as those we have been sketching here pay too much attention to the world and not enough to the Word of God. Barth repudiated all natural theologies (attempts to arrive at knowledge of the existence and nature of God in ways that are logically independent of revelation or faith) and apologetic theologies (theologies which emphasize the need to make the Christian faith understandable to particular historical and cultural settings). In either case, Barth believed, the theologian is likely to give authority to something other than God's own self-manifestation.

Theology's warrant, Barth argued, is the Word of God, God's revelation. Theologians do not interpret the Word of God, however, for that Word, as God's, is never available to us as a possession or a fixed object. It is grace, which is God's free and sovereign act. The Word of God has the character of event, not of ideas. The fullest and most decisive embodiment of God's Word is the event of Jesus Christ, who was and is the Word of God, God Incarnate. The theologians' task is to interpret the witnesses, and that means the scriptural witnesses, for the canonical documents are testimonies to the preparation for the coming of Jesus Christ and the history of Jesus Christ which proved themselves to the early centuries of the church by the efficacy of their witness (Barth 1963, 26–36).

Because God's Word has the character of *event* in and over which God remains sovereign and free, it is not known in academic objectivity, but only in faith and by the aid of the Holy Spirit. Because it is this living Word which is the real subject to which the Scriptures bear witness, the Scriptures too are understood only in faith and by the aid of the Holy Spirit. Thus, faith— which is not just believing in doctrines or in God, but can be spoken of as en- counter with the one in whom one believes—is an indispensable precondi- tion of the work of theology. But that does not mean, Barth insisted, that faith is the subject of theology. In his view, that supposition is one of the ma- jor mistakes of much modern theology. Theology is faith seeking under- standing, but it is the Word of God, not its own faith, which theology seeks to understand.

Barth's emphatic focus upon the Word of God in the event of Jesus Christ as proclaimed in the witness of Scripture was the basis for his criticisms of both "conservative" and "liberal" theologies. Theologies which identify any particular doctrinal formulations or even the words of Scripture themselves with the truth make the grave mistake of denying God's sovereign freedom over God's Word, denying its character as "living." But so also, in Barth's judgment, do theologies which let modern philosophies, anthropologies, or world views lead to a rejection of such scriptural affirmations as the virgin birth of Jesus and his resurrection (ibid., 103).

Here we confront directly the issue concerning questions about "how God acts." Barth was insisting that any affirmation concerning God, if it is to make claim to being a Christian affirmation, must be based upon God's self- communication. Above all else this is in the event of Jesus Christ, and our ac- cess to that is dependent upon the scriptural testimonies. Christian faith un- derstands through those witnesses that Jesus Christ was God's self-giving reconciling act, a free act of God's sovereign love. It is, therefore, a supernat- ural act, not an act subject to the laws of nature or explainable within the cat- egories of any human philosophy. This "ultimate mystery" of God's choice to take human nature into unity with God's self in order as "very God and very man, to become the Word of reconciliation spoken by God to man" is the sole point of origination of the New Testament witness and therefore of any Christian understanding of revelation (Barth 1956, 124). It is a miracle.

> It comes to us as a *Novum* which, when it becomes an object for us, we cannot in- corporate in the series of our other objects, cannot compare with them, cannot deduce from their context, cannot regard as analogous with them. It comes to us as a datum with no point of connection with any previous datum. (Ibid., 172)

Barth had no wish to hide behind ambiguities in the word "miracle," such as the legitimate translation of the German word *Wunder* and the New Testa- ment word *téras* as "wonder" instead of the common translation as "miracle," thus suggesting events which are awe-inspiring but are not necessarily caused by supernatural interventions. In the same context we have quoted here, Barth went on to discuss the affirmation of the virgin birth.

But now let us turn to the main point, *ex virgine*. What is meant by that? Certainly the general and formal fact that the becoming, the actual human existence of the Revealer of God who is God Himself, . . . is a miracle. That is to say, it is an event in this world of ours, yet such that it is not grounded upon the continuity of events in this world nor is it to be understood in terms of it. . . . We ought not to be content merely to make clear its discontinuity, its "supernaturalness." Miraculous and marvellous are two different things. (Ibid., 187)

The point to be made here is not simply *that* Barth affirmed supernatural interventions by God, but *why* he affirmed them and repudiated the theologies which do not. It was his conviction that the Christian faith was established by the miraculous event of the incarnation of the Word of God in Jesus Christ who was true God and true man. It follows that the denial that God acts, when God chooses to do so, by supernatural intervention is a denial of Christian faith. And more specifically, there can be no Christian theology that does not affirm the miracle of the two natures (true God and true man) of the Incarnate Word.

Although these few paragraphs can only begin to suggest the character of Barth's theology, they may serve to illustrate not only the difference between modern theologies which affirm the traditional Christian belief in divine intervention and those which judge that we should reformulate our understanding of our faith without that affirmation, but also the difficulty of adjudicating this difference. From the standpoint of the more traditional theologies, those theologians who seek to interpret Christian faith without divine interventions have "thrown out the baby with the bath water." Their nonmiraculous interpretations of the act of God in Jesus Christ deny the freedom and sovereignty of God and the character of salvation as God's unconditioned gift. In their elevation of modern experience to the status of an authority requiring basic revision of the witness of Scripture and tradition, they implicitly deny the role of the Holy Spirit in the community of faith.

From the standpoint of the modern theologians who are thus charged, the foregoing accusations are not only untrue, but "question-begging." They judge that they are not denying God's grace and revelation, but seeking to distinguish between what is from God and what is from the human witnesses and interpreters. Modern historical science has shown, they believe, that the biblical witnesses proclaimed their faith in terms of the understandings which were given with their cultural and historical settings. The assumption of divine interventions on the part of the biblical witnesses was inevitable, and in itself it constituted no offense to its hearers. To insist today, however, that their cultural assumptions are essential aspects of God's self-giving makes no more sense than insisting that the gospel can be understood only in Aramaic or Greek, and it confronts today's hearers with an offense other than that of the gospel. Such an insistence does not challenge us to let go of our sinful self-centeredness and accept God's grace, but to let go of our experience of the world and accept an ancient and alien world view.

Put in terms of logic, Barth's arguments against these theologies "beg the question," for they *presuppose* one answer to the very question in dispute between them. All of Barth's arguments *assume* supernatural causal intervention as their basis and authority. *If* God has wrought the salvation of humankind by the miracle of the incarnation of God's Word in Jesus Christ as interpreted by the Council of Chalcedon, *then*, without doubt, the theologies which seek to interpret Christian faith without appeals to supernatural causal interventions are wrong. But how does one remove the "if" and establish the premise? Barth argued that Chalcedon correctly interpreted the New Testament witnesses. But even if one granted that much-debated point, it does not answer the question—*unless* one assumes that Scripture's interpretations also transcend historical and cultural relativities with an authority rooted in supernatural causal intervention! Barth did not argue in this way. He recognized that his arguments, suggested above, presupposed his theological perspective. As he expressed this in one context, "One cannot subsequently speak christologically, if Christology [as Barth was affirming it] has not already been presupposed at the outset, and in its stead other presuppositions have claimed one's attention" (ibid., 123).

To point out that Barth's arguments—if treated as valid refutations of these theologies—"beg the question" is not to say that Barth's theology is wrong. It is only to point out that they do not show the other theologies to be wrong. By the same token, the argument that "modern experience" shows theologies like Barth's (which insist upon the affirmation of divine interventions) to be wrong also begs the question. From Barth's standpoint the granting of such authority to "modern experience" is an assertion of human judgment over against divine revelation.

It should be noted that although the specific affirmations attributed to Karl Barth here are not all agreed to among the many modern theologians who continue to affirm supernatural causal interventions, the basic argument is usually the same. In one way or another, the criticism of theologies that reject supernaturalist appeals is rooted in an *assumption* of just such supernaturalist appeals. As Barth suggested, this is a disagreement involving the basic judgments with which one begins to do theological work. It is not a question, however, as sometimes claimed, of whether one will listen to God or to human judgments, for it is a question in either case of human judgments as to what constitutes listening to God.

The question as to whether Christian faith entails the affirmation of supernatural causal intervention or not is one of the most important issues dividing modern theologians. Every aspect of method and every doctrine are deeply affected. So also are the practical issues regarding ethics, the problem of evil, and the relationships between Christians and persons and peoples of other religions. This issue cannot be settled independently, however. It illustrates the importance of historical and cultural relativity for theology, entails one's judgment regarding the nature of Scripture, and cannot be dealt with separately from the questions concerning the meaning and nature of revelation and the problem of theological authority which are examined in the next chapter.

WORKS CITED

Barth, K.
    1956   *Church Dogmatics.* Vol. 1, part 2. Translated by G. T. Thomson and H. Knight. Edinburgh: T. & T. Clark.

    1963   *Evangelical Theology: An Introduction.* Translated by G. Foley. New York: Holt, Rinehart & Winston.

Ford, L. S.
    1970   "The Viability of Whitehead's God for Christian Theology." In *Philosophy and Christian Theology,* edited by G. F. McLean and J. P. Dougherty; *Proceedings of the American Catholic Philosophical Association* 44:141–51.

Kaufman, G.
    1968a   "On the Meaning of 'Act of God.'" In *Harvard Theological Review* 61:175–201.

    1968b   *Systematic Theology: A Historicist Perspective.* New York: Charles Scribner's Sons.

    1971   "What Shall We Do With the Bible?" *Interpretation* 25, no. 1: 95–112.

    1972   *God the Problem.* Cambridge: Harvard University Press.

    1975   *An Essay on Theological Method.* Missoula, Mont.: Scholars Press.

    1981   *The Theological Imagination: Constructing the Concept of God.* Philadelphia: Westminster Press.

Neville, R.
    1980   *Creativity and God: A Challenge to Process Theology.* New York: Harper & Row.

Ogden, S.
    1963   *The Reality of God and Other Essays.* New York: Harper & Row.

    1979   *Faith & Freedom: Toward a Theology of Liberation.* Nashville: Abingdon Press.

    1982   *The Point of Christology.* New York: Harper & Row.

Schleiermacher, F.
  1928   *The Christian Faith*. Edited by H. R. Mackintosh and J. S. Stewart. Edinburgh: T. & T. Clark.

Tillich, P.
  1951   *Systematic Theology*. Vol. 1. Chicago: University of Chicago Press.

Whitehead, A. N.
  1926   *Religion in the Making*. New York: Macmillan Co.
  1929   *Process and Reality: An Essay in Cosmology*. New York: Macmillan Co.

Williams, R. R.
  1978   *Schleiermacher the Theologian: The Construction of the Doctrine of God*. Philadelphia: Fortress Press.

3
REINTERPRETING REVELATION AND AUTHORITY

IT IS VERY difficult today to appreciate the enormous authority exercised by the churches during the several centuries preceding the onset of our "modern era." It extended not only over beliefs and morality, but also over law, education, art, science, and philosophy. This power was undergirded by the common assumption that church authority was rooted in the authority of God whose will was known to the church because of *revelation*.

REINTERPRETING REVELATION

Just what was understood by the term "revelation" is not, however, easily summarized. It was assumed, but it was not clarified. It was not a matter of theological focus, because the broad general assumption was not seriously challenged. It can now be seen that both in the Scriptures and throughout the history of developing Christian doctrine there were varying themes concerning the nature, the content, and the means by which God was understood to have communicated with persons, and no unified interpretation was sought or established.

Even the life-and-death struggle between the Protestant Reformers and the defenders of traditional Roman Catholicism did not bring forth a theological focus on the meaning of revelation, for both sides assumed that God was in some mysterious way the real source of the authorities to which they appealed. Underlying their disagreement about authority was an assumption about revelation which was, in essence, common to both.

The Protestants insisted upon the sole authority of the Scriptures, affirming that God was the author of the Scriptures and provided there everything that humankind needed. Increasingly, during the succeeding post-Reformation generations, the biblical documents were seen as a body of revealed truths given by God.

The Roman Catholic position, as declared by the Council of Trent in 1546, was that the truths necessary for salvation and the moral teachings required for the Christian life were contained in the Scriptures *and* in the traditions in which the church maintained the unwritten teachings of Christ to the apostles. To this difference regarding the authority of tradition may be added the Catholic insistence upon the authority of the church as interpreter of Scripture and tradition.

Those differences were of great importance, but the basic understanding of revelation was the same for both Protestants and Catholics. The *content* of revelation was understood to be *revealed truths* given miraculously by God. What God gave in revelation was information about the divine nature and will—and many other things presumably related thereto. For both groups God was understood as a being outside the creation acting upon it supernaturally, revelation being but one form of that action, and the dominant understanding of faith for both during these centuries (sixteenth, seventeenth, and eighteenth) was that it is intellectual assent to the (allegedly) revealed truths.

Developing Doubts Concerning Propositional Revelation

Propositional revelation, as this understanding is called today, did not, however, receive its full and explicit doctrinal formulations until the late nineteenth and early twentieth centuries. This development was partly in response to the growing impact of the modern world view in general, but it came more in response to the "modern" theological developments which this work is discussing. Among these was a variety of reinterpretations of revelation that explicitly repudiated the idea of propositional revelation as incompatible with the gospel. Two of the influential reinterpretations and then a current defense of propositional revelation are sketched in this chapter.

The proponents of each of these views contend that their interpretations are motivated by a concern for loyalty to the gospel as it is conveyed by the biblical witnesses. It is also clear, however, that these doctrines developed in response to the challenges presented to Christian theology by the cultural revolutions which led to the modern world. Galileo's observations showed the scriptural understanding of the cosmos—as interpreted by the churches —to be mistaken, and the impact of the new scientific method, the essential elements of which are first brought together by Galileo, effectively discredited the traditional church-dominated methods of gaining knowledge. Modern philosophy arose in the rethinking of this problem of knowledge, and, especially in the works of Hume and Kant, led to conclusions that were quite incompatible with the assumption of propositional revelation, casting serious doubt on the applicability of human concepts to the understanding of God and therewith upon the very possibility of having knowledge of God. Continuing developments in the natural sciences gradually made clearer the historical and cultural relativity of the biblical world view and showed that the basic concepts that had been assumed in Christian descriptions of the nature, activity, and will of God were not even adequate for describing the scientifically observable world.

Reflecting the cultural impact of the new approaches to knowledge, the application of historical-critical study to the Scriptures has increasingly led Christian scholars to the conclusion that those documents do indeed manifest historical and cultural relativity and other characteristics of the humanness of their authors and editors. Further, the biblical documents have been judged to have been "kerygmatic" in intention. The primary purpose of their authors was not to convey information but to evoke the response of faith.

All of these developments cast doubt on the idea of propositional revelation. The efforts of representatives of the churches to maintain the literal and/or factual accuracy of various biblical passages—on the assumption that they had been given word for word by the supernatural activity of God— increasingly brought further doubt as the new methods produced more convincing interpretations of such things as the relative movements of the "heavenly bodies," the causes of disease, or the explanations of apparent discrepancies in the texts and the manuscripts. Although increasing numbers of persons have concluded that the Bible is a collection of ancient documents without authority for the modern world, modern theologians have rejected this judgment and have argued that the fault is not in the Scriptures but in the ways in which they have been defended and interpreted. In particular the modern theologians have concluded that the nature of revelation and the relationship of revelation to the biblical writings have been misunderstood.

Revelation as Personal Encounter

Revelation is not the giving of *information* but God's *self*-giving. Such is the insistence of a wide variety of contemporary theologians in opposition to both conservative and liberal rationalisms. One of the most influential forms of this general position earlier in this century was the teaching of Swiss theologian Emil Brunner (1889–1966) that revelation should be understood as "personal encounter." Indeed, not only revelation but also faith and truth are to be understood in terms of personal encounter.

Brunner argued that in the person Jesus Christ we meet God as Person, and we come to "know" God personally. Knowing a person is basically different from knowing about a person. I might know *about* you without knowing you. In that case we have no personal relationship, and though I may recognize that you are a person, for me you are an "object" of my knowing. Just how compatible these two kinds of knowing are in a relationship between two human beings is a matter of much disagreement. In our usual relationships, both are present, so we assume that they are readily complementary. We also recognize, however, that to have information about persons without any personal acquaintance is *not* to know them. Our impressions, based on the information, may have given us a very distorted view of them. But even if we avoid prejudicial conclusions, the fact remains that we do not know them.

In propositional revelation it is supposed that God has given information about the divine will, actions, and nature (as well as about many other subjects). The "knowledge" of God provided here is knowledge *that* God is this or that, wills such and such, has done so and so. Even if it asserts that "God is love," and that it is God's will that we trust in that love, one's *believing* these things in one's mind does not constitute a loving relationship. Indeed, one may accept these teachings intellectually and with firm commitment and yet remain quite alien from God, experiencing God's presence as essentially oppressive. In such circumstances those who *believe* (intellectually) that God is love but do not accept that love personally are mistaken in that very belief because they misunderstand the teaching. To understand the affirmation that "God is love" one must be personally encountered by that love, experience being loved, and trust the divine Lover.

Brunner was affirming that revelation, faith, truth, and human beings are all to be understood "relationally." *Faith* is the human response of obedient trust in the gracious personal presence of God. Belief in—intellectual assent to—assertions about God is not faith and has its usefulness only as an adjunct to the personal relationship. *Revelation* is first of all God's act of self-giving; it is God's gracious personal presence to persons. God is "revealed" when the response of faith to God's self-giving enables persons to enter into the personal encounter, the loving relationship, which God offers. The *truth* given in revelation is the living presence of God as personally known in the encounter. Any subsequent statement such as that one has been encountered by the loving presence of God is *not* itself the truth. It is a human attempt to bear witness to the happening of truth in the encounter. Hearers of that witness will know the truth to which it would point only if they participate in that encounter.

This thoroughgoing opposition to "objectivism" led to the charges that Brunner was espousing "subjectivism" and that no doctrines, no interpretations of the meaning of the revelation, were possible on such a basis. In response to the former, Brunner argued that both "objectivism" and "subjectivism" are wrong from the standpoint of faith. The understanding of revelation as personal encounter, itself but a human attempt to bear witness to the event and not a claim to be the truth itself, is not in any way an affirmation that revelation comes from the human being. Quite the contrary, it witnesses to the experience of being graciously encountered, forgiven, affirmed, re-created, and sustained. The experience of revelation is one in which the human beings recognize themselves to have been met by a transcendent Other and discover themselves—in the faith relationship—to be open to and caring for other persons far more truly than ever before. All of this is anything but "subjectivism" (Brunner 1964, 65–85).

Still, if the truth cannot be captured in doctrines because it has the character of personal encounter—that is, if what is given in revelation is not information but God's gracious Self—can there be Christian doctrines? The answer is, of course, yes, provided that "doctrine" is understood in a manner consistent with the understanding of revelation, faith, and truth as personal encounter.

Faith, not belief but obedient trust in the gracious God by whom the faithful have been encountered, is the presupposition of the possibility of theology. Faith is not, however, the subject of theology. The subject of Christian theology is God encountered as Person in the person of Jesus Christ. The reality of this holy and gracious presence is known (personal acquaintance) because it is a matter of experience. But that is no objective and impersonal datum. Faith "knows" God as Person, as gracious, as sovereign, as Lord, indeed, as Creator, for these are ways of understanding and bearing witness to faith's experience. To affirm the reality of God as Creator is not to make a statement about some scientifically inferable cosmic event. It is to express faith's experience of the utter trustworthiness, and therefore the sovereignty, of that personal love by which the faithful have been encountered. By contrast, to live with the sense that God is not the transcendent source of all that is (other than God) and therein with the sense that there are aspects of reality over which God is not sovereign is to live outside of that utter trusting obedience which is faith, outside of the relationship which is the presupposition of understanding the truth which theology seeks to serve.

The general understanding is the same with the doctrine of the Trinity. It is not some strange and incomprehensible formulation of the objective inner being of the Deity.

> For this is just the meaning of the mysterious doctrine of the Tripersonal God: God as he is by and in himself, in his unfathomable mystery, is none other than he who has manifested himself in his revelation in Jesus Christ as the Lord and as the loving Father. The doctrine of the Trinity, the doctrine of the everlasting love of the Father for the Son and of the Son for the Father through the Holy Spirit, attacks the notion that God as he is "by himself" is another than God as he is "for us" in his revelation. . . . God wills—even when we think about him as he is in himself—to be known as no other than the One who meets us in Jesus Christ, his Son, as the God who approaches man, the God who would communicate himself and who in his self-communication glorifies himself. (Ibid., 141)

The point Brunner is making here is not that the doctrine of the Trinity gives objective information about the inner being of the Deity. Rather he sees that doctrine as faith's affirmation that God—as self-disclosed—is completely trustworthy. Because faith is such personal obedient trust, it is confident that the mysterious, holy, transcendent Thou is not other than the loving One who has encountered us.

If theology is so thoroughly grounded in the revelation-faith relationship, might this not suggest that the theologian needs only to attend to the Holy Spirit, the living presence of God, and can dispense with the Scriptures? For Brunner the answer to this question is emphatically no! It is the witness of the community of faith (the church) to its having been encountered by the personal God in the person of Jesus Christ which has evoked the event of revelation-faith for the continuing community of faith, including the theologians. This witnessing is dependent upon the witness of the Scriptures. It is that witness which enables the encounter with Jesus Christ in every subsequent generation. That witness is therefore indispensable and authoritative.

Nevertheless, Scripture is constituted by the witnessing of faithful human beings. There is no possibility of identifying the specific words of the Bible with God's truth itself. God is that truth. For us it is "truth as encounter." To regard any set of human statements (propositions), whether the words of the Bible or the Creeds or any other, as identical with God's truth would be to reject God's gracious presence and commit idolatry.

Even on the basis of so brief a description of Brunner's doctrine of revelation as personal encounter it should be possible to understand its impact upon the issues that have been raised for Christian theology by the cultural revolutions which have led to the modern world. To a large extent those problems of apparent conflict between Christian faith and the modern world view arose because of the assumption that revelation is a miraculous source of information contained in the propositions of Scripture, creed, and tradition. If revelation is reinterpreted as personal encounter, this whole situation is changed. Since what is given in revelation is God's gracious presence and not information, and the Scriptures are understood to be human attempts to convey to others the wondrousness of that transforming encounter, there is not only no need to affirm the idea of biblical inerrancy and to cling to the world view of those ancient peoples but it is also seen to be essential to recognize that the words and concepts of the witnesses are not the content of God's revelation. There is no difficulty in accepting the historical and cultural relativity and the humanness of all witnesses. Nor is there any basis for the supposition that the prescientific assumptions of those witnesses are part of the content of the revelation. Revelation is not concerned, for example, with whether or how species have evolved. It is a gift received in a personal encounter in which it is "known" that the species, however they have reached their present states, are all God's creatures, having their being from and within God's grace.

Such a reinterpretation of revelation and Scripture thus immediately removes much of the apparent conflict between Christian faith and modern experience, but it does not simplify the tasks of interpreting Scripture and tradition. The interpreters (which, in principle, should include all persons of Christian faith) must struggle with the distinction of the content of the revelation from the culturally and humanly relative formulations. In Brunner's view, that content is only "understood" when the interpreter participates in that personal encounter to which the formulations have borne witness. That those formulations have made such subsequent encounters possible shows their validity and justifies their continued authority in the community of faith. Nevertheless, the authority is not in the specifics of the formulations. It is in the communicating of the event of revelation—as personal encounter. Its result is not new information but a new life set free by love for love, a love which will heal on the Sabbath, and which will be willing to suffer and die for all neighbors.

Brunner's interpretation of revelation has been very influential but also much debated. It is described here as illustrative of a type of modern understanding of revelation. Few theologians today would espouse Brunner's position in its details. Most judge that Brunner placed too much weight on the idea of "personal encounter," and suggest that it is at best but one of many metaphors which can be employed in the effort to convey the character of Christian religious experience. Yet there is also much general agreement of perspective in various modern theologies that revelation is God's gracious self-giving "known" in the responsive relationship of faith.

The issue of God's agency, whether or not God acts by supernatural causal intervention, is one of the basic points of disagreement among such theologians. Brunner affirmed that God does intervene, most specifically in the incarnation which made possible the personal encounter with God in the person of Jesus Christ. However, the understanding of revelation as a relationship of grace/faith does not require either the affirmation or the denial of that traditional view of God's active presence. Indeed, it readily lends itself to an understanding of the effective presence of God without causal interventions, as has been indicated in the previous chapter.

This general approach to the understanding of revelation is not, however, the only modern alternative to the traditional assumption of propositional revelation. One of the most influential and emphatically different views is the emphasis upon history itself as revelation.

Revelation as History

Some emphasis upon historical events such as the exodus and the incarnation is an aspect of most Christian interpretations of revelation. Yet for the proponents of propositional revelation the primary and essential body of revelation is the written forms, especially the Scriptures. It is this to which we have access, and it is these writings that tell us both the facts and the meanings of those historical events. For proponents of views like the understanding of revelation as personal encounter, those historical events were vehicles of the event of revelation in the personal encounter. The meaning of such events is only grasped by way of participation in the encounter, because the reconciled relationship is their meaning.

Particularly in the twentieth century, several theologians have argued that history is the primary category for understanding revelation. Archbishop William Temple (1881–1944), for example, contended that the understanding of God as Creator implies that every thing and every occurrence is in some degree an expression of the will of God ("natural revelation"), and that the belief in God as Personality entails the judgment that under special circumstances God will act in special ways that will be especially revealing of the divine nature and will ("special revelation") (Temple 1956, 301–7). Yet, in his view, these primary acts of revelation in historical events need the supplement of a secondary form of God's revealing activity "in the illumination of the minds of prophets to read those events as disclosing the judgment or the purpose of God" (ibid., 312). This was not, however, an affirmation of propositional revelation. Archbishop Temple was emphatic in his rejection of any such view as incompatible with faith and with the character of Jesus' teaching (ibid., 311). In revelation "there is no imparting of truth as the intellect apprehends truth, but there is event and appreciation; and in the coincidence of these the revelation consists" (ibid., 314).

While Temple was arguing here in a rather philosophical fashion—as required by the lectureship under whose auspices this material was presented—others have contended for the primacy of history in the understanding of revelation on biblical grounds. The Old Testament scholar G. Ernest Wright (1909–74) wrote that ". . . Biblical theology is *the confessional recital of the redemptive acts of God* in a particular history, because history is the chief medium of revelation" (Wright 1952, 13). The lives, the acts, and the experiences of individuals are aspects of revelation in history, he said, but they are "mediate means" and not the center of God's acts which "are more inclusive and comprehensive than the words, works and inner life of any one personality" (ibid.). Because it is these "mighty acts of God in history" that constitute the essential reality of revelation, the words of the Bible are *not* to be identified with God's revelation. It is the historical events that are the revelation, and human words can never fully capture the reality and meaning of those happenings. The Bible is narrative and confessional in form, proclaiming God's saving acts in which the divine purposes are manifested. It has been a basic error of subsequent theologies to emphasize doctrinal formulations which so thoroughly abstract from the living reality of God revealed in the saving events (ibid., 32). Biblical theology is "recital," not dogmatic system. Wright also repudiated understandings of revelation that place primary emphasis upon the inner experience. "To be sure, God also reveals himself and his will in various ways to the inner consciousness of man, as in other religions. Yet the nature and content of this inner revelation is determined by the outward, objective happenings of history in which individuals are called to participate" (ibid., 55). Thus, although he was appreciative of some aspects of Brunner's teachings, Wright judged an understanding of revelation that places primary emphasis upon the personal encounter to reverse the true priority and lose the biblical perspective.

Like Temple, Wright saw a need for the interpretation of the historical events that faith saw as the saving acts of God, and he affirmed the role of the prophets in explaining the divine intention and meaning of the revelatory events. It is not clear, however, how much Wright agreed with Temple concerning the illumination of the interpreters as a secondary form of revelation. On the one hand, Wright wrote that the "source of their enlightenment was not from mystical experiences but from history itself and from the character and purpose of God revealed in both past and present." But, on the same page, he also affirmed that ". . . when God acted, he also 'spoke' in numerous ways, but especially by chosen interpreters" (ibid., 83).

Although the relationship between event and interpretation is not clear, and Wright did not develop a clarification of what he meant by "act of God," it is evident that, like Temple, he was affirming supernatural causal intervention as the basis for his view of revelation as God's saving acts in history. Here again, the repudiation of propositional revelation and biblical inerrancy is not due to a "modernist" disbelief in miracle, but to a different reading of the Scriptures.

A distinctly different emphasis upon the category of history in the interpretation of revelation is seen in H. Richard Niebuhr's book *The Meaning of Revelation*. Niebuhr (1894–1962) denied that the events of revelation are "there" objectively in the historical events themselves and avoided any appeal to miraculous interventions. Revelation, he argued, is not a matter of *external history*, but of *internal history* (Niebuhr 1941, 90, 154). In the former we deal quantitatively and impersonally with objects. In the latter subjects and values for persons are central. Here again, the authority for such an emphasis is the Scriptures. Niebuhr agreed that the biblical witnesses found the inspiration for Christianity in history, but he insisted that they did not deal with history as spectators. Their accounts were "confessional," proclaiming the meaning of events for persons responding in faith, not a meaning to be seen in the events apart from this personal involvement. In order to understand the scriptural accounts of historical events, one must see them as the witnesses saw them. "One must look with them and not at them to verify their visions, participate in their history rather than regard it if one would apprehend what they apprehended" (ibid., 73).

The central and decisive event for Christian faith and community is the event Jesus Christ. For Christian *faith* this is the event in which the God of all events is revealed as self. It is the event that illuminates all of life and history—but only for faith. "Revelation as the self-disclosure of the infinite person is realized in us only through the faith which is a personal act of commitment, of confidence and trust, not a belief about the nature of things. . . . The God who reveals himself in Jesus Christ is now trusted and known as the contemporary God, revealing himself in every event; but we do not understand how we could trace his working in these happenings if he did not make himself known to us through the memory of Jesus Christ . . ." (ibid., 154).

Niebuhr's view thus brought together both the emphasis upon history as the vehicle of revelation and "personal encounter" as an essential aspect of the content of revelation. The emphasis upon "internal history" that makes this joining of motifs possible also provides the basis for a nonsupernaturalist understanding of revelation and with it the judgment that Christians can and should expect that the God known through faith's witness to the divine self made known in our particular history is actively present in every time, event, and community (ibid., 87). Supernaturalism and exclusivism go together and are abandoned together.

Niebuhr's interpretation of revelation in terms of "internal history" has been very influential in twentieth-century theology, but its rejection of objectivism has been opposed by many, including the most prominent representatives of a more recent insistence that it is history itself, indeed objective history, which is God's revelation. The best-known representative of this perspective is Wolfhart Pannenberg (b. 1928).

Pannenberg agrees with the judgment that revelation is not a supernatural gift of information, but God's self-disclosure, and like all the other theologians whose views on revelation have been discussed here he bases this judgment—in part—on what he perceives to be the nature and witness of the Scriptures (Pannenberg et al. 1968, 4, 13). But he emphatically rejects personalistic understandings of revelation such as Brunner's with their affirmation of a *direct* disclosure of God's Self. Instead, he contends that God gives an *indirect* self-revelation in history, and not just *in* history, for it is history as a whole, the whole of history, which discloses who God is, and thus *it is history itself which is the revelation* (ibid., 13).

In affirming that all of history is—without supernatural causal intervention—expressive of the living presence of God, Pannenberg is in agreement with some of the theologians discussed in the previous chapter. His view that the totality of history is itself God's self-revealing activity is similar to Gordon Kaufman's interpretation of the whole of history as "God's master act." The distinctiveness of Pannenberg's position can be seen in his answers to several questions which his doctrine of revelation raises: (1) Why must it be history in its totality in order to be revelation? (2) How can there be any such revelation, then, since history is unfinished? (3) What becomes of the Christian conviction that Jesus Christ is God's decisive revelation? Interestingly, the answer to the second question is also the answer to the third.

Pannenberg gives two answers to the first of these questions. (1) He contends that any individual event can illuminate the being of God in no more than a partial way, while revelation in its "strict sense" must be a full disclosure of the divine essence. The latter claim here is not really explained or defended so much as asserted on the authority of the philosopher Hegel. One can, however, see weight to the argument that particular events by themselves would seem at best to offer no more than very ambiguous indications of the nature and will of the sovereign Creator (ibid., 5, 16). (2) He argues that the Scriptures themselves manifest such a view. This is implicit in the fact that the Old Testament's witnesses to revelation of Yahweh are provisional. There are always new events whose meanings surpass the earlier. This is no longer true in the New Testament, for reasons which appear in the answers to the second and third questions (ibid., 140–41).

To insist that only the whole of history can be revelation in the "strict sense" of the term would seem to deny revelation altogether, since history has not yet run its full course, and when it has, revelation will either be impossible or unnecessary—or both. Pannenberg (and others) find an answer to this problem in attention to the relationship of two biblical emphases: (1) the Hebrew expectation of God's ending of history in the final judgment, and (2) the resurrection of Jesus Christ. The former, which manifests the effort to see history as a whole, made possible the recognition of the latter, the resurrection, as the decisive beginning, the inbreaking, of the end of history. "It is only in the course of this history brought about by Jahweh that this tribal God proves himself to be the one true God. This proof will be made in the strict and ultimate sense only at the end of all history. However, in the fate of Jesus, the end of history is experienced in advance as an anticipation" (ibid., 134). That is to say, because of their expectations of God's ending of history, some of the Jews were able to recognize in the resurrection of Jesus the "inauguration" of that divinely given end and thereby to see history as a whole. This then is truly revelation. In seeing history in its totality they were seeing the God who gives and guides it.

The viewpoint is more clearly seen when it is understood that in Pannenberg's judgment the resurrection is a thoroughly objective event. This is not to say that he believes that the appearances of the risen Jesus were of such a nature that they could have been photographed (had the equipment been available), but he argues that modern secular historiography can establish that Jesus was raised from the dead (Pannenberg 1968, 88–106). The resurrection in no way depended upon the faith of the disciples. It was an event that happened to Jesus and that made possible the faith of the disciples. By the action of God, Jesus was transformed (ibid., 66, 100). Because some of the disciples actually were confronted by appearances of the risen Jesus, their faith in God is grounded in knowledge. Pannenberg argues that faith which is not thus based on knowledge of the being of God is gullibility or superstition (Pannenberg 1967, 130–31). The resurrection of Jesus is not simply something in which one believes blindly, but an event which "is open to general reasonableness" and speaks "the language of facts" (Pannenberg et al. 1968, 137).

It is this rational objective knowledge of the resurrection of Jesus that justifies faith in him as the decisive manifestation of God. Jesus' teaching and deeds, no matter how mighty, "could not show unambiguously whether Jesus personally was the one in whom salvation or judgment are [sic] ultimately decided" (Pannenberg 1968, 64). The resurrection did provide this full and unambiguous verification. This knowledge is the presupposition of faith. Faith as belief and trust in God is based on the objective knowledge of God's reality, nature, and purposes provided by revelation. That revelation is history itself which can be seen in its essential wholeness because of the resurrection of Jesus. What is given in revelation is, again, not information, but God's self-disclosure, but it is given in "external history" (using Niebuhr's distinction), and—contrary to Niebuhr and Brunner—provides an objective knowledge. For Pannenberg, knowledge of God is the presupposition of faith. For Brunner and Niebuhr, faith is the presupposition of "knowledge" of God.

Nevertheless, for Pannenberg also, the scriptural witness upon which we are dependent is not freed from humanness and historical and cultural relativity. The doctrines of biblical inerrancy and propositional revelation are repudiated, yet in its affirmation of objective certainties and faith as based on intellect, this view of revelation as history is much closer to the conservative orthodoxies than are the others discussed above.

No doubt this brief description of Pannenberg's view of revelation raises a host of further questions, but the concern here is not to give either a full explication or a critical assessment of the views being described. It is rather to illustrate the ways in which modern theologians are reinterpreting revelation. Here again, the reading of the Scriptures and the impact of the modern world combine to evoke the conviction that revelation is not the miraculous impartation of information but the self-manifestation of God. The Scriptures are therefore seen as human and historically and culturally relative witnesses to the living presence of God with and in history. That both the Scriptures and the traditional teachings of the churches manifest the limited perspectives and understandings of the times and cultures within which they were formulated does not deny their value and importance, but it does call for a recognition of the continuing need for reformulating our understandings of the nature and will of God in and for our own times and struggles. With all of the disagreements among modern theologians, there is nevertheless this much underlying agreement. It is not, however, an agreement shared by all persons teaching and writing in the field of theology today!

Continuing Defenses of Propositional Revelation

There are many Christian scholars today, both Protestant and Roman Catholic, who resist the "modern theology" which is being described in this work. Probably the clearest single point of this resistance is in their defenses of the idea of propositional revelation. The theological positions being described here are not to be identified as Fundamentalist. Most of the "conservative" or "orthodox" or (as they often refer to themselves) "evangelical" theologians today are critical of Fundamentalism, seeing it as rigid, narrow, anti-intellectual, and "biblicistic" rather than truly biblical.

As scholars, these theologians know that the evidence of the available manuscripts makes it impossible to claim that any version of the Bible as we now have it is "inerrant." In affirming modern historical-critical biblical scholarship, many of them restrict this affirmation to text criticism, and remain skeptical (at best) about source, form, tradition, redaction, and canon criticism, and other forms of modern biblical study. In their judgment, these approaches to the Scriptures "beg the question" by assuming the methods of modern historiography which exclude the possibility of discerning the transcendent and the supernatural. Other evangelical scholars take what might be called a "cautious" stance toward the various methods of critical scholarship. Bernard Ramm (b. 1916), for example, calls for "reverent biblical criticism," and he warns at the same time against the dangers of naiveté and gullibility.

> It is very important that the Church have a strong sense of the right and wrong, the historical and fictional, and truth and error in treating the Bible as a document. Otherwise the Church is no better than the cult or sect or religion which hesitates to bring the strongest light of knowledge to bear on its documents but rather canonizes them with its own self-imposed (albeit human and erring) authority. The fear of a destructive criticism must be balanced with a fear of gullibility and credulity as exhibited by the cultists and sectarians. (Ramm 1961, 192)

As this statement illustrates, the continuing affirmation of the Scriptures as a written form of God's revelation by evangelical scholars is not an expression of a naive or simplistic point of view. To begin with, such scholars do not reduce divine revelation to written statements. They affirm several forms of revelation, including nature, historical events, visions, dreams, the inspiration of the prophets, and above all, the incarnation. They find these and others affirmed in the Scriptures, yet they emphasize the primacy of the written form. Some, like Carl F. H. Henry (b. 1913), are more emphatic about this than is Ramm.

> Some evangelicals who espouse propositional revelation hesitate nonetheless to say that God's revelation is expressed or conveyed exclusively in a rational and objectively true form. They affirm instead that, in addition to God's frequent and possibly even normal conveyance of revelation in propositional form, God sometimes discloses himself in other than propositional modes. They emphasize that the biblical terminology of revelation sometimes suggests features not reducible to propositional statements but that are correlated rather with dreams and visions and imagery. But, it should be indicated, the extraverbal and extrarational belong only to the rim of revelation; revelation in its essential definition centers in the communication of God's Word. (Henry 1979, 457)

Although there are many such differences among "evangelicals" (even some who reject propositional revelation), there is far more agreement among them than there is between them and the theologians who are being described as "modern" here. Most of them agree, for example, that *for us* the primary form of revelation is the written (or propositional) form. Against those who emphasize historical events as the essential form of revelation, they insist that, apart from revelation given in words, events are not understandable. Even the crucifixion of Jesus Christ would have remained ambiguous for us apart from special revelation in words (Ramm 1961, 78).

The disagreement with the emphasis upon "personal encounter" as the essential content of revelation is more complex, because there is *some* agreement. It is agreed that faith must include every aspect of a person and not just conscious reason, and it is agreed that there should be personal encounter with Jesus Christ. But it is argued that in including every aspect of the person faith must include objective knowledge and that there could be no personal encounter with Christ without the special revelation that comes in words. A viewpoint like Brunner's is therefore seen as a false dichotomy, wrongly disparaging words in the comparison with the personal relationship (ibid., 146–47). Something as intangible as a "personal encounter" provides no clear basis for sound doctrine. "Putting it directly, if divine revelation is truly revelation it must reach the human race in a substantial form. It must come as speech or language and bearing a rich conceptual booty with it. Because there is truth in revelation there are truths of revelation" (ibid., 151). As Henry puts it, "While to contrast divine self-revelation with divine propositional revelation seems to promise a superior kind of noncognitive revelation, it actually succeeds only in opening a door to subjectivity" (Henry 1979, 459).

For us today, in distinction from the prophets and from the disciples, the available form of this language of revelation is the Scriptures. The words and statements of the Bible are not just human witnessing, for they are believed to be inspired by God. "Inspiration, then, is the Holy Spirit securing for the Church the Christian *graphe* [something written] in such a form that the Church may trust its verbal form as an adequate, authentic, and sufficient vehicle of special revelation" (Ramm 1961, 179). Ramm argues that this does not conflict with the affirmation that the writers of Scripture were real authors. Somehow, in a way beyond our understanding, the Holy Spirit guided those writers in their selection of words without reducing their humanity in that process. The Scriptures, he says, are the result of a dual authorship, and neither the role of the Holy Spirit nor that of the apostles infringes upon that of the other. This is a mystery (ibid.).

The crucial difference, then, between supporters of propositional revelation (Ramm does not approve of this phrase) and opponents of it is not that the former deny that there is revelation in history, or that there is personal encounter in revelation, or that Jesus Christ is the very heart of God's revelation, or that revelation is God's self-disclosure. The difference is that the defenders of propositional revelation argue that all of the former would fail if revelation were not *also* in verbal form, that is, if certain statements in human language were not themselves a part—for us the primary part—of the very content of what is revealed. The opponents of such a view, by contrast, contend that all such words, those of Scripture, creed, tradition, and doctrine, manifest such historical and cultural relativity and other human limitations as to show that they are human witnessing to revelation, but not the revelation itself. The "evangelical" view affirms that Christians have divinely authorized statements which provide correct information and doctrines as truths given by God. The "modern" view contends that revelation is the gracious self-giving of the Truth which God *is* and which we can never therefore have at our disposal, never possess. In having faithful but fallible human witness and interpretation, we are challenged to trust in that sovereign grace and to take responsibility for continual reinterpretation.

It would be incorrect to suggest that the defenders of propositional revelation take no account of historical and cultural relativity. Because it is believed, however, that God's revelation is given in language, it is understood that the statements—even though they must reflect cultural relativities—are nevertheless controlled by God's revealing activity. God "condescends" in revealing, but it is still God's revealing and therefore the truth (ibid., 39–40). It is not claimed that this assurance removes all problems of interpretation, though in practice it seems to allow very little room for departure from one's own tradition's interpretations.

As noted in earlier contexts in this work, this disagreement is very difficult to adjudicate. The "evangelical" position begins with the conviction that the traditional assumption of propositional revelation is correct, and it defends that assumption by appealing to it. The "modern" approaches argue that an examination of the Scriptures themselves shows that those documents are not in fact what the premodern assumption supposed. But, as the defenders of that tradition would point out, in examining the Scriptures from a would-be neutral observer's standpoint using the tools of modern historiography, one has ruled out beforehand the possibility of discerning the Word of God therein. The critical theologians' rejoinder is that while this can happen, it need not. It is possible to approach the Scriptures and traditions in faith, knowing as a matter of experience that their witness and interpretations have made that faith possible, and to examine those documents humbly asking *how* they have functioned in this process. And so the argument continues! "Argument" seems to be the right word here, for it is rarely a discussion. This disagreement marks a major division within Christendom.

Agreements and Disagreements Concerning Revelation

In his very helpful book *Models of Revelation,* Avery Dulles describes five different general understandings of revelation that are being proposed by contemporary theologians, both Roman Catholic and Protestant, only three of which are represented in the foregoing discussion. That the current disagreements about revelation are more complex than is shown in this chapter is certainly true, and Dulles's book is commended for those who would pursue the subject. Nevertheless, Dulles believes that it is possible to offer the following statement as an expression of general agreement among many proponents of each of the five "models": "Revelation is God's free action whereby he communicates saving truth to created minds, especially through Jesus Christ as accepted by the apostolic Church and attested by the Bible and by the continuing community of believers" (Dulles 1983, 117). Even though the suggested agreement is less than might at first appear, since key words (e.g., truth, attested) would have to mean significantly different things to representatives of the different interpretations of revelation in order for all to affirm the statement, it still represents an important amount of common ground.

Nevertheless, as Dulles goes on to point out, and as the discussion in this chapter has illustrated, there are genuine incompatibilities among the several doctrines. They are by no means all strictly between the "propositionalists" and the "nonpropositionalists." For the purposes of this study, however, that disagreement is of particular concern, for it is indicative of a *general* difference between "modern" and traditional theologies, and it has important implications for yet further contrasts between the two. One of these is the issue of "authority" in theology.

REINTERPRETING AUTHORITY

It would be easy to conclude from the foregoing discussions that modern theology has no firm basis on which to make affirmations about the nature, the activity, and the will of God. This is the opinion of the "evangelical" theologians, and it *seems* to be confirmed by such modern theologians as Edward Farley and Peter C. Hodgson who judge that "with the end of mythological thinking about God, the theological foundations of the scripture principle evaporate. . . . The house of authority has collapsed, despite the fact that many people still try to live in it" (Farley and Hodgson 1985, 76). This judgment, which in varying degrees and expressions is shared by many modern theologians, results from much critical reflection on the historical developments and cultural changes that this work has been describing. It does not, however, indicate agreement with the view that modern theology has no adequate basis for its reinterpretations. Indeed, the collapse of "the house of authority" is not lamented but praised, for it is the conviction of such modern theologians that the kinds of authority claimed by and for the traditional theologies are incompatible with Christian faith (ibid., 61–86). The claims were idolatrous, their effects were oppressive and dehumanizing, their character was contrary to the will of God manifest in Jesus Christ.

This last assertion illustrates an *apparent* contradiction in "modern" theology. The traditional assumption concerning biblical (and traditional and ecclesiastical) authority is being rejected on the basis of a conviction concerning the manifestation of God in Jesus Christ. Such an argument entails a dependence upon Scripture, tradition, and church—at least implicitly. Whether or not such an argument is self-contradictory depends upon the nature of that "dependence." If one were to assert that the traditional assumptions of the authority of Scripture (and/or tradition, church) were contrary to the manifestation of God in Jesus Christ simply because Scripture (or tradition or church) "says so," that would clearly be a case of appealing to the very kind of authority that is being denied. Instances of this contradiction (usually less blatant) can indeed be found in modern theological writings, but they are a careless violation rather than an example of the conclusions of modern theologians.

The Interdependence of Scripture, Tradition, and Church

Modern theologians in general share some basic conclusions about "authority" for theological judgments. First among these is that the Scriptures have either *a* or *the* primary role. That role, however, though primary is neither simple nor isolated. It is entangled—inevitably—with tradition and church, and appeals to these three factors entail the involvement of faith, reason, and experience in any self-critical process of theological reflection.

As these generalizations imply, the traditional Protestant claim of *sola scriptura* (that the Scriptures *alone* are the authority for theological judgments) has been abandoned by modern Christian theology. It is recognized by both Protestant and Catholic theologians that the Reformation and post-Reformation debates pitting appeals to the authority of Scripture against appeals to the authority of tradition were based on misunderstandings produced by the severity of that struggle. The most obvious point of misunderstanding is the fact that Scripture and tradition are inseparable and not even easily distinguishable. The Scriptures are a part of tradition. They came into being within the ongoing life of the communities of faith (that is, within "church" and "tradition"), were chosen and designated as Scriptures by the ongoing processes of the living community of faith (that is, by "church" and "tradition"), and have been maintained (copied, translated, interpreted, employed as authoritative) in and by that same complex community.

Certainly one may point to a particular canon in some currently available form and say that those documents are "the Scriptures" and thereby distinguishable from "tradition" (defined in such a way as to exclude these documents) and from "church," no matter how defined. But this very act of distinction affirms a complex variety of acts by church and tradition, such as the acceptance of these documents into the life of various communities of faith, the decisions of various councils regarding which documents are "canonical," the production of copies and translations, and the development of interpretations that kept the documents meaningful in the ever-changing circumstances of those communities. So powerful have these influences of church and tradition been that those who suppose that they can "hear" the Scriptures without regard to tradition are more subject to tradition than are those who recognize and work critically with its roles in relation to Scripture. It is frequently evident (except to themselves) when such persons appeal to the "clear teaching of Scripture" that they are in fact "hearing" what particular traditions have taught them. At the very least, one needs to pay serious attention to the history of the interpretation of Christian faith in order to be able to assess critically the ways in which one's own "hearing" of the Scriptures has been influenced by tradition. Without tradition we would neither hear nor have the Scriptures.

Nevertheless, the distinction of Scripture from tradition, though not an absolute distinction, is an important one. The Christ-event, though subject to varieties of interpretation, is what brought the community of Christian faith into being, and the Scriptures are our primary means of access to that event. The New Testament writings show dependence upon the earliest Christian traditions. That *those* traditions were in this literal sense prior to the writings that were eventually to be regarded as Christian Scriptures hardly justifies, however, the judgment that tradition in general is now either prior or equal to those Scriptures. Since it is the Christ-event that is decisive in our history, the New Testament, as the closest available means of access to that event, is necessarily our primary *source*, and its witness is in some sense both normative and authoritative.

Jesus Christ as Primary Norm and Authority

The qualification "in some sense" is required first of all because in Christian theology it is Jesus Christ who is the primary norm and authority. The belief in the verbal inspiration and inerrancy of all canonical writings rendered this distinction (of revelation in Jesus Christ from revelation in Scripture) unimportant, but its reappearance did not come first with modern biblical scholarship. Most notably, Martin Luther made critical judgments concerning the books of the Bible, evaluating the degree to which they proclaimed Christ. The Christ of whom he learned through those very Scriptures (understood in terms of Luther's doctrine of justification by grace) was the norm for these judgments. The application of this norm meant that for Luther not all of the books of the New Testament had the same authority. It is, however, modern historical-critical scholarship that has made this distinction both essential and difficult.

It is essential, for the documents have been shown to be human, historically and culturally relative, and kerygmatic. They are not themselves the "Word of God," even though we are dependent upon them for our knowledge of the Incarnate Word of God. The importance of the witness is not in itself but in that to which it bears witness. The distinction is essential.

But modern historical-critical scholarship has also shown the distinction to be difficult. It is now recognized that the New Testament does not include any direct eyewitness accounts of the Christ-event, and its writings do not seek to give merely factual accounts of the life and ministry of Jesus of Nazareth. They tell about Jesus of Nazareth, proclaiming that he is the Christ, but they do so on the basis of prior accounts and proclamations in and for particular new contexts and situations. They thus offer contextual theological reinterpretations. They do not provide us with simple direct access to Jesus of Nazareth. Among scholars there is general agreement that the question of how much knowledge we can have concerning "the historical Jesus" is a very difficult one, and there is much disagreement among the specific answers proffered. How then can Jesus Christ be the primary norm and authority in Christian theology?

This is not as severe a problem as it may sound at first, if one notes that the reference is to *Jesus Christ*. The term "Christ" is a title, an interpretive theological title. It indicates a response of faith on the part of anyone using it appropriately. The point is that it is not a neutral observer's objective description of Jesus of Nazareth which constitutes the norm for Christian theology, but Jesus confessed as the Christ perceived by faith. The latter, not the former, is what the New Testament offers. Certainly it is understandable that persons of Christian faith and persons who are struggling with the decision as to whether or not to make that commitment want to know as much as possible concerning "just what he was really like," but this desire is often entangled in the mistaken assumption that objective factual description could establish whether or not Jesus was the Christ. Because that is actually a question about God, asking whether God was decisively present and active in and through this man, Jesus, no amount of factual data will fully answer the question. In theory, such data could show this claim to be false (if, for example, there was evidence that Jesus was an "evil" person), but they could not establish objectively that the claim is true. As noted above, some modern theologians such as W. Pannenberg reject this judgment.

This does not mean that persons of Christian faith live in a state of basic uncertainty. That would, indeed, indicate an absence of faith, unless the meaning of the term "faith" is reduced to some very limited involvement of the self, such as a mere intellectual assent to doctrines or an arbitrary and irrational emotional attachment. Such uses of the term have usually been deemed misunderstandings or distortions, for faith is commonly understood by the theologians to involve every essential dimension of the self, to entail basic change in persons, a fundamental change toward greater wholeness, and to include participation in a community of faith. Thus, for persons of faith there is experiential evidence that Jesus is the Christ. By participating in that community of faith that came into being in response to the proclamation that Jesus is the Christ, Christians experience the truth of that proclamation. They "know" that Jesus has effectively established the inbreaking of "God's kingdom," has inaugurated the community of freedom in grace, because they participate in that community. But this is only "knowledge" by participation. It "proves" nothing to the nonparticipating observer. It seems fair to say that a great many of those who call themselves "Christians" do not share in this experience either, and that makes the claim all the less persuasive to the observer. It does not, however, remove the experience and its assurance from those who do participate therein.

In this discussion of "authority" in Christian theology there are three points to be noted. The first is the point stated above, that it is Jesus Christ who is the primary norm and authority in Christian theology rather than Scripture itself, even though this establishes a decisive authoritative role for Scripture because of our dependence upon Scripture for knowledge of Jesus Christ.

The second point is that this authority for Scripture is not limited to the New Testament, and the role of the Old Testament is not reduced to that of providing necessary background for understanding Jesus Christ and the New Testament. Usually modern Christian scholars (in agreement with tradition) affirm that the Old Testament also bears important witness to the living presence, the nature, and the will of God. Like the New Testament, the Old Testament teachings are judged by the norm of Jesus Christ.

The third point is that this discussion has also introduced an important role for religious experience into the questions about authority in theology. If faith (as described above) is a presupposition for understanding the affirmation that Jesus is the Christ and thus for any Christian understanding of the kerygmatic witnessing of the Scriptures, then that religious experience (faith) is an aspect of authority in theology. This would not simply be as a precondition for understanding the authorities of Jesus Christ and Scripture, for the *experience* of being forgiven, accepted, loved, set free from captivity to one's anxious self-protectiveness, and so on, would inevitably play a significant role not only in how one "hears" texts but also in how one understands Jesus Christ and in how one will judge assertions regarding the nature, the activity, and the will of God.

The Role of Reason

Thus far in this discussion of the reinterpreting of authority in Christian theology it has been noted that the Scriptures have a primary role in the establishing of theological conclusions in modern theologies, but that the Scriptures do not serve alone as the authority, because they are inevitably entangled with tradition, church, and religious experience. To these four factors must be added at least two others: reason and general experience.

To concede the obvious necessity of using reason in the making of theological judgments might be only to acknowledge reason as an instrument, but not as an authority, and there are some who would hold to that limitation. It has sometimes been argued that to give human reasoning the status of an authority in theology is clearly to manifest the human pride that is unwilling to accept humbly God's revelation—however the latter is defined. And sometimes this argument is supported by appeals to such passages of Scripture as Paul's affirmation of "the foolishness of God."

For the word of the cross is folly to those who are perishing, but to us who are being saved it is the power of God. For it is written,
   "I will destroy the wisdom of the wise,
   and the cleverness of the clever I will thwart."
Where is the wise man? Where is the scribe? Where is the debater of this age? Has not God made foolish the wisdom of the world? For since, in the wisdom of

God, the world did not know God through wisdom, it pleased God through the folly of what we preach to save those who believe. For Jews demand signs and Greeks seek wisdom, but we preach Christ crucified, a stumbling block to Jews, and folly to Gentiles, but to those who are called, both Jews and Greeks, Christ the power of God and the wisdom of God. For the foolishness of God is wiser than men, and the weakness of God is stronger than men. (1 Cor 1:18–25)

Apart from the fact that in modern theology it is agreed that one can no longer presume to settle a disagreement by a traditional authoritarian appeal to a text (evidently presuming propositional revelation, ignoring contexts, etc.), such an appeal here would miss the point under discussion. Modern Christian theologians do not argue for reason as an authority over against or instead of revelation. Christian theology is a reflective task carried on within the community of faith whose existence arose in response to the grace of God decisively manifest in Jesus Christ. The priority of God's gift is beyond question. God is *the* authority, but God does not do the work of the theologians. (Some may be tempted to say, "Thank God," suggesting that we would be better off without theology, until they note that this would imply that Christians have no responsibility to understand, obey, and proclaim God's "will.")

The question here is not whether reason is an authority instead of or over against Scripture, for example, but whether reason is in some important sense an authority in Christian theology in addition to and in conjunction with Scripture, tradition, church, religious experience, and any other factors which may be found to enter in. Is reason an essential part of the basis upon which one theological conclusion is judged superior to another? Clearly, it is reason which makes such judgments, and it does so not just on the basis of the number of texts of Scripture that appear to support one view rather than another. Given faith's conviction of the trustworthiness of God, reason infers that God is neither self-contradictory, nor capricious, nor essentially inconsistent, nor a deceiver. Careful examination of such judgments will reveal authority roles for Scripture, tradition, church, and religious experience, but also a dependence upon "the canons of reason." No inference is possible without them, and therefore no theology. Reason's "law of noncontradiction" (among others) is being employed, and it is inescapably an element of authority in Christian theology.

The acknowledgment that reason must be recognized as an authority in theology in addition to Scripture, tradition, church, and religious experience has long been present in Roman Catholic theology, but it is hardly new in Protestant theology in spite of the polemics associated with the *sola scriptura* formula. John Wesley (1703–91), for example, affirmed the four interdependent authorities (or norms) of Scripture, tradition, experience, and reason. Dennis Campbell (b. 1945), in a recent study of authority in American theology from Jonathan Edwards (1703–58) to the present time, concluded that

Historical study of authority for theology indicates that the reciprocally dynamic nature of the relationship between authority and Christian community does in fact give rise to a rich complex of norms by which the church lives and in terms of which theological construction is undertaken. These have usually been Bible, creed, tradition, inner experience, and reason. The intertwined and functionally variable character of these authoritative elements means that no singular theological interpretation can ever be reached; it also means that the question of authority must be antecedent to any serious theological work. (Campbell 1976, 108)

Multiple Mediate Norms

Campbell speaks of this "rich complex of norms" as multiple "mediate" norms (ibid., 97, 103). They are "mediate" because God and only God is the absolute authority. Campbell further argues that it would be unwise to try to establish any strict formula for priorities among the several norms or authorities because of the great differences among the particular questions on which they must be brought to bear in theological reflection and because of the danger of "rigidification" which might "sap the vitality of faith" (ibid., 114). It would appear that there is widespread agreement on these points in modern theology.

Campbell's list of authorities differs slightly from the one developed in this chapter. Here "creed" has been assumed as an aspect of "tradition," though a case could be made for its separate treatment, and Campbell does not include "church" in his list, but speaks of "the reciprocally dynamic nature of the relationship between authority and Christian community," which acknowledges that that community (church) is an authority factor in Christian theology. Protestants have resisted claims that the church is an authority in theology because of their historic perception of Roman Catholicism as an authoritarian freedom-denying monolith, an institution which has sought to take God's place in human lives. Whatever degree of truth there may have been at one time or another in this unbalanced description, however much less true it is since the Second Vatican Council, and how much the same description might apply to some Protestant churches are all beside the point being made by Campbell or in this discussion. The notion of the church as an authority in modern theology does not imply that theologians should submit their formulations to one or another of the institutions which are called churches. It is the elusive and difficult-to-define "community of faith" that is intended. Campbell states the case for its inclusion in the understanding of authority as follows:

Historical study of authority for theology suggests that there is an inseparable relationship between authority and the community of faith. Christian community is never set over against the "sense of the heart," though the institutional church may be. Christian faith can become real only for the individual, but it can become real only for the individual in the context of community where the shared experiences of past and present Christians amplify and correct one's own experience. It makes no sense to talk of a person of Christian faith apart from the community upon which he is dependent and to which he is accountable. (Ibid., 96)

Campbell does not name "church" as an authority, but as the "context" for theology which is authoritative (ibid., 97). The distinction he is making is probably that church is not one of the factors which theologians can employ critically and systematically in making theological decisions. It is an authority which functions before, during, and after the theologians' efforts. In the longer term, it is the response of the community of faith that "decides" which proposals for theological reinterpretation are to contribute meaningfully to the ongoing life of the church. On this general point, there is widespread agreement in modern theology. The community of faith is in fact an authority in theology, but because of its own elusiveness, it is not a factor employed "systematically" by the theologians.

The Role of General Experience

There is yet another important authority factor for modern theologies that is not included in Campbell's list. This is what may be called "general experience" as distinguished from "religious experience." The term "general experience" is intended to include not only the common ways of experiencing of persons living in cultures that have been changed by the impacts of modern science, technology, education, transportation, communication, and so forth, but also the scientific experiences (discoveries) themselves. There is much continuing reluctance to grant that such "secular" sources of knowledge and conviction could be authoritative in Christian theology, but it is clear that they are. Campbell acknowledges this when he says,

one who reads the Bible must bring judgment and insight to it in order to receive the biblical word. This judgment and insight derives from Christian experience, from church teachings, and *from the reality of life in the world.* (Ibid., 111, italics added)

The ways in which we interpret the meaning of the affirmation that God is the Creator have been changed by discoveries in astronomy, physics, and biology. Some will still argue that these things have involved no correction of any biblical assertion, but only of (mis)understandings of those ancient texts regarding the origins and age of the cosmos, of the species, and so forth. But even that concession would grant to scientific learning a role as an authority in theology. This effort to maintain the doctrine of scriptural inerrancy has been rejected by modern theology. It is acknowledged that the biblical authors were human beings who interpreted the events of revelation/faith in terms of their own historical and cultural relativities. It is affirmed that the truth to which they bore witness transcends those relativities and that the interpreters must struggle to distinguish that truth from the "earthen vessels" in which it has been conveyed. This sometimes involves the judgment that those biblical witnesses were mistaken in their interpretations. For example, it is clear that various biblical authors understood the "final judgment" to be an objective event that was to happen within the lifetime of their own generation. General experience has shown that to be mistaken, and on this and other issues has in fact functioned as an authority in Christian theology.

One still hears claims of *sola scriptura* in the theological literature, but it is increasingly acknowledged that *as a matter of fact* there are—as there must be—several authoritative factors at work in the making of theological judgments. The *primacy* of Scripture is maintained by most Christian theologians, but it is recognized that interpretation of the scriptural witnesses is appropriately influenced by tradition, church, religious experience, and even by general experience. Theologians must struggle with the questions concerning how each of these should be understood and applied in relation to each other on any particular theological question. There is no agreed-upon formula, and it is likely that none is possible today—if ever.

Illustrating the Use of Multiple Authorities: Gender Consciousness in Theology

Consider, for example, the question about whether it is appropriate to speak of God as "He" or as "She," as "Father" or "Mother," and the like, which has recently become a matter of considerable concern. Some have been inclined to try to settle this question by the appeal to "Scripture alone," and this has usually involved the judgment that since the Bible speaks of God as masculine in a great many ways, with great frequency, and without apology, then clearly God should be spoken of in masculine terms. Others, implicitly making the same appeal to the assumed unique authority of Scripture, could point out that there are some biblical references to God in feminine terms. For example, Deut. 32:18, Isa. 42:14b, and Isa. 66:13 all liken God to a mother. Clearly the preponderance of references is masculine, but to suppose that one could settle a theological question by such a method of citation of texts would be to assume propositional revelation, deny the historical nature of the Scriptures, and, in effect, repudiate both modern scholarship and contemporary experience. One might argue that such a criticism assumes authorities in addition to Scripture, thus begging the question. But the begging of the question is really on the other side, for one of the questions here is how the Scriptures are to be interpreted. The assumption of propositional revelation is caught up in the theological circle as much as is any other view.

Sometimes "tradition" is added to Scripture, and here again the far-greater weight of usage has been masculine. The practice of the churches has embodied this masculine priority in ways which show that it has not been merely a

linguistic convenience to use masculine terms for the Deity. But these familiar appeals to tradition or to Scripture and tradition also ignore the historical
character of both.

Much has been learned in the *general experience* of the modern era, including discoveries in both the natural and the social sciences, that bears on this
question. In particular, it is now evident that both the scriptural and the traditional male orientations in theology were reflective of cultural assumptions
of the superiority of males that are no longer defensible. There are indeed differences between men and women, and they are not simply physical differences, but there is no basis for claims that either is inherently superior to the
other in intelligence, insight, wisdom, creativity, or any other expression of
the "spiritual dimension" of human being. It is also clear that sexist structures in society are dehumanizing. Thus, the cultural biases that can be seen
to be reflected in the scriptural and traditional preferences for male designations of God were an expression of ignorance with destructive consequences.

Christian *religious experience,* in spite of the common cultural biases, has included an awareness of divine characteristics that the same cultures have
judged to be "feminine" in addition to the more "masculine" ones. God has
been "known" as compassionate, patient, willing to suffer, and so on, and
not just as powerful, authoritative, demanding, and so forth. Indeed there is
much at the very heart of the Christian gospel proclaiming a forgiving and
suffering Messiah that has been resisted by the masculine-oriented cultures
of our history.

Reason recognizes the inconsistency between faith's experience of God's
utterly trustworthy graciousness and the incompleteness and insufficiency of
a being who can properly be described as "male" *or* "female" or even as both.
Both are partial, incomplete, each needing the other to be what it is as well as
to fulfill the functions of sexual differentiation. To suppose that God *is* male
(or female, or a mere combination of both) is to affirm an "idol," to depict as
utterly trustworthy something which, being finite, incomplete, and dependent, cannot bear the weight of faith.

Thus far this sketch of ways in which the "multiple mediate authorities"
might be seen as relevant to this question would appear to cast Scripture and
tradition aside. That is, however, a misleading impression resulting from the
fact that the references to the authority of Scripture and tradition have been,
so far, reflective only of their traditional and precritical uses. When the human and historical characteristics of the Scriptures are recognized and the assumption of propositional revelation is given up, one will not try to establish
theological conclusions by any mere citing of texts. One will rather participate in the efforts to "hear" the truth that transcends the particularities of the
formulations of those human and historical witnesses. Certainly we are all fallible in our efforts to distinguish between the historical and cultural biases of
the witnesses and the reality of God's grace, and we, too, are human and his-

torical creatures who must offer interpretations and bear witness in particular historical, linguistic, and cultural settings. That, however, is hardly an argument for avoiding the effort to make the distinctions and propose reformulations in each "here and now." As explained in chapter 1, one of the differences between modern and premodern theology is the far-greater degree to which these relativities are recognized and self-critical efforts are made to allow for them.

Increasingly today Christian theologians judge that the witness of Scripture (and tradition) to the love of God for all creatures is incompatible with both sexually limited conceptions of God and sexist social structures. Both can be seen to be dehumanizing in their effects, and thus contrary to the grace of God of which we have learned through those historically and culturally relative human witnesses to the embodiment of God-for-us in Jesus Christ. This judgment indicates that our conceptions and symbolizings of God need to include and transcend both the masculine and the feminine. It does not yet offer specific answers to the questions about how to do this doctrinally or liturgically. Complex questions regarding religious and theological language and meaning must be considered, as will be discussed in the next chapter.

It is not to be expected that readers will be persuaded by this illustrative sketch of any conclusions about this issue that they had not previously reached. The purpose here is only to indicate how the several authority factors are, in fact, at work in the ongoing processes of theological reformulation.

Modern theologians are recognizing increasingly that "the house of authority has collapsed" (Farley 1982, 165–68). Neither theologians nor ecclesiastical institutions can reasonably claim the right today to "possess" revelation or grace in such a fashion as to assert definitive authority over the beliefs and conduct of individuals and communities. It is not simply that churches do not in fact have such authority, but that, viewed theologically, they have no right to such authority. The grace of God is, by definition and experience, both free and beyond our full comprehension. It frees persons of faith to take the responsibility of proposing reinterpretations in and for the community of faith. When this is essayed by modern theologians, it is done with the recognition of "multiple mediate authorities" (Campbell 1976) and with the hope that the proposals will be tried and refined in the fires of the theological community and the life of the church.

WORKS CITED

Brunner, E.
   1964   *Truth as Encounter*. Translated by E. W. Loos and David Cairns. Philadelphia: Westminster Press.

Campbell, D. M.
1976   *Authority and the Renewal of American Theology.* A Pilgrim
                Press Book. Philadelphia: United Church Press.

Dulles, A.
1983   *Models of Revelation.* Garden City, N.Y.: Doubleday & Co.

Farley, E.
1982   *Ecclesial Reflection: An Anatomy of Theological Method.* Phila-
                delphia: Fortress Press.

Farley, E., and P. C. Hodgson
1985   "Scripture and Tradition." In *Christian Theology: An Introduc-
                tion to Its Traditions and Tasks.* 2d ed., rev. and enl., edited by
                P. C. Hodgson and R. H. King, 61–87. Philadelphia: Fortress
                Press.

Henry, C. F. H.
1979   *God, Revelation and Authority.* Vol. 3, *God Who Speaks and
                Shows. Fifteen Theses, Part Two.* Waco, Tex.: Word.

Niebuhr, H. R.
1941   *The Meaning of Revelation.* New York: Macmillan Co.

Pannenberg, W.
1967   "The Revelation of God in Jesus of Nazareth." In *Theology as
                History,* edited by J. M. Robinson and J. B. Cobb, 101–33.
                New Frontiers in Theology, vol. 3. New York: Harper & Row.
1968   *Jesus—God and Man.* Translated by L. L. Wilkins and D. A.
                Priebe. Philadelphia: Westminster Press.

Pannenberg, W., R. Rendtorff, T. Rendtorff, and U. Wilkens
1968   *Revelation as History.* Edited by W. Pannenberg. Translated by
                D. Granskou. New York: Macmillan Co.

Ramm, B.
1961   *Special Revelation and the Word of God.* Grand Rapids: Wm. B.
                Eerdmans.

Temple, W.
1956 [1934]   *Nature, Man and God.* London: Macmillan & Co.

Wright, G. E.
1952   *God Who Acts: Biblical Theology as Recital.* Studies in Biblical
                Theology 8. Chicago: Henry Regnery.

4

REASSESSING LANGUAGE, MEANING, AND TRUTH IN THEOLOGY

LANGUAGE IS THE medium in which theological formulations are wrought. This is nothing unique to theology, for language is an essential vehicle for almost everything which may be judged to characterize humanity (science, politics, religion, literature, morality, sociality, humor, etc.), and though we know of complex systems of communication among various other creatures and capacities in some to learn to employ limited vocabularies of human language meaningfully, the degree to which human life may be described as linguistic clearly distinguishes human beings from all other creatures—as we now understand them. Indeed, some have argued that the human being may best be defined as the linguistic animal. It seems clear that language is at least *an* essential human characteristic.

Yet while language enables so much that is human and is thus a great source of freedom, it is also a "prison" that sets limits to human freedom. Language enables us to think, to calculate, to understand, to plan, and to communicate. Yet whatever particular language (or languages) we employ restricts our capacities for all of these purposes. As some have expressed it, a person or a society lives in a "language world." We do not ordinarily realize this, however, for our language is so inescapably the precondition for human experiencing and understanding, being that *through which* all of our experience is filtered and *by which* our understandings are structured, that we fail to take note of it. We naturally, but naively, suppose that our formulations comprehend the real as it is in itself rather than as it is filtered by our language and the concepts expressed therein. Recent discoveries in the natural sciences, such as the wave/particle duality in the "behavior" of photons and electrons, have made clear that the limitations of our languages and concepts are important in the understanding of finite realities and not just in fields like philosophy and theology where the understanding of ultimates is sought.

TRADITIONAL APPROACHES TO THE PROBLEM
OF TALKING ABOUT GOD

The realization that there are serious problems involved with human attempts to talk about God is hardly new. It is recognized in Scripture and throughout the history of theology, though it seems often not to have been recognized in popular religion. The reality intended by words such as "God" has been understood by prophets and theologians to be "transcendent," that is, beyond the limits (structures) that characterize everything other than God. The monotheistic religions have not just affirmed that the one true God is the greatest of all finite beings, but that God is the source, the Creator, of all finite beings. The structures that constitute their being and their finitude are also from God. God has therefore been spoken of in such terms as "immortal," "invisible," "infinite," "eternal," and "ubiquitous." Such talk sounds at first as though it constitutes a definite understanding of God. But note that while the word "definite" suggests a setting of limits, the words in question are denials of limits: not mortal, not visible, not finite, not temporal, not spatial. Certainly God has also been spoken of in positive ways such as that God is holy, God is gracious, God is love, God is Spirit, and so forth. In these cases, however, we have terms for which we cannot establish clear definitions. One might argue that we can "understand" what love is by experiencing it, even if our definitions are inadequate, and that therefore when we speak of God as love we make a positive and understandable assertion. The problem is not escaped so easily, however, unless one is willing to affirm that the love we experience is precisely what we wish to affirm regarding God, that is, that human love and divine love are the same, or perhaps that our experience of God's love and our understanding of that experience are equivalent to that reality itself. God's love has traditionally been qualified as "infinite" in order to remind us of the presumption involved in such a claim.

The Negative Way

One of the influential answers to this problem that has appeared in various periods of the history of Christian doctrine is known as the *via negativa*, the negative way. Its proponents have argued that we cannot make proper affirmations regarding God. Statements that appear to be affirmations are ways of saying that God is greater than what can be said or thought. Therefore, according to this point of view, the better theologies deny that God is wise, or powerful, or loving. In doing so, they are not suggesting that God is less than the wisdom, power, or love which we understand, but confessing that God is so much more than these that we cannot truly describe God in such terms— or in any of our words and concepts.

The Way of Analogy

This "pessimism" regarding the possibilities for speaking affirmatively of God has not been shared by most of the theologians. Far more influential has been the way of *analogy*. Making affirmations about God by way of analogy has been seen as an answer to a dilemma. On the one hand, if we suppose that the terms we use to describe God have the *same* meaning as when they are employed to describe creatures (*univocal predication*), we will be denying the divine transcendence and at best be describing an "idol." On the other hand, if, acknowledging the divine transcendence, we hold that the terms as applied to God have essentially different meanings than they have when used to refer to creatures, we will be admitting to the fallacy of "equivocation." The affirmations will only mislead by giving the appearance of meaningful statements when in fact the meaning in relation to God is different from the meaning we understand from our observations of the creatures. Thus the meaning of the statement in relation to God remains unknown.

Analogical predication steers between these two unacceptable extremes. The claim is that even though there is a difference between the meaning of a term as applied to God and as applied to anything else, there is sometimes also some likeness or proportionality. If we say "God is good," we recognize that the meaning of "good" here is not the same as its meaning when we say the weather is good or even when we say that a person is good. That does not mean, however, that the meaning of "good" as applied to God is utterly different from its meaning in these other contexts. It is both different and similar. The goodness of any creature is limited; that of God is not. Our understanding of goodness is also limited, so our understanding of God's goodness is partial. Yet, according to the doctrine of analogy, such a partial understanding is surely meaningful.

In general, an analogy is simply a likening of two things, a claim that the two are similar and that therefore if we understand one of them, we can understand the other on the basis of that similarity. In a more technical sense, an analogy is a comparison in terms of relationships. The clearest form is mathematical, such as 2:4::6:x (two is to four as six is to the unknown). Thus, it is evident that x = 12. If someone says "He is like a father to me," this is an implied analogy suggesting that the speaker experiences his or her relationship to the person referred to as being similar to the relationship a person has with his or her father. Of course, this father analogy has been an important one in reference to God in Christian tradition.

Clearly, there are difficulties with this kind of answer to the problem of speaking meaningfully of God. Even in the strictly human uses of this analogy there is the difficulty that different persons have very different experiences in relations with their fathers (which is also true of other familiar analogies for God such as "Judge," "Lord," "King," etc.). An analogical reference to God involves yet greater problems, for, as compared with the mathematical analogy, the theological analogy has two unknowns (God and the characteristic being predicated of God). Thus, while in the mathematical example the facts that three of the four elements are clearly understood and that the fourth is understood to be entirely of the same kind make it possible to grasp the fourth element clearly, in the theological use neither the reality of God nor the characteristic analogically ascribed to God is clearly known or commensurable with the first two (because of the divine transcendence). Can a theological analogy be supposed, then, to provide more than a vague suggestion of meaning regarding God? This continues to be a subject of considerable debate. The "classic" formulations of the doctrine of analogical predication concerning God are those of Saint Thomas Aquinas, yet today there is much disagreement among defenders of Aquinas's teachings on analogy regarding their correct interpretation (Tracy and Cobb 1983, 21–25) and their adequacy for the problem.

MODERN APPROACHES TO THE PROBLEM
OF TALKING ABOUT GOD

Questions about the meaningfulness of "God-talk" have arisen more frequently and more urgently in the modern era. Each of the cultural revolutions that contributed to the development of our modern world (see *Understanding Modern Theology I*) posed questions about theological language and meaning, and these questions have been seen to complicate the issues in modern theology discussed in the foregoing chapters of this volume. Perhaps the most direct challenge to claims that we can speak meaningfully of God came from the modern philosophical movement known as "linguistic analysis," which itself arose in response to the impact of modern science upon culture.

Empiricist Approaches

A group of scholars brought together by the physicist Ernst Mach in Vienna toward the end of the last century observed that in the empirical sciences progress is made, whereas in fields like theology, ethics, and metaphysics no such progress is to be discerned. In such nonempirical fields the old debates continue even though varieties of proposed answers continue to appear and to create new divisions among us. The discussions in this group, which came to be known as "the Vienna Circle," led to the judgment that the reason for this contrast in the development of these different fields of study was the empiricism of the former and its lack in the latter. Their proposal was not that empirical methods (appeals to sense data) provide *knowledge*, but that they are the basis for *meaning*. A natural scientist can understand precisely what is meant by another scientist who announces a new finding, because he or she can carry out the same observations and/or experiments that the first followed to arrive at the announced conclusion. By contrast, when theologians or philosophers of different schools of thought or different religious bodies disagree in their proclamations of the will of the one good God or their interpretations of the nature of reality, there is no adequate way in which the disagreements may be resolved, for there is no way of testing the meaningfulness of their assertions. So, at least, insisted the scholars of the Vienna Circle. They concluded that empirical verifiability is the essential condition for meaningfulness. If a statement can be tested by observations (or if we can see how it will become possible to test it) so that it can be shown to be either true or false, it is to be judged meaningful. Otherwise it is not meaningful. It is nonsense. Statements such as "There is a God," "One ought to tell the truth," or "Reality is like mind" may express feelings, but they are not meaningful. The only statements besides those which are empirically verifiable or falsifiable which—according to this theory—may be judged meaningful are tautologies, statements that repeat in the predicate what is already present in the subject.

Meaning as Verifiability

The philosophical movement that began with this proposal for bringing greater clarity into human affairs by distinguishing between meaningful statements and nonmeaningful ones by means of empirical testing was known in its early forms as "logical positivism" or "logical empiricism." Its general spirit (usually called "positivism") is still encountered in various forms.

One professor of philosophy, for example, challenges his students' uses of religious language with an illustration like the following. Imagine a friend (we will call her "Mary") who claims to have an invisible pet elephant. She has given it a name. Let us say "Elizabeth." Mary tells us that she and Elizabeth are such close friends that they are inseparable. She may also tell us, on occasion, that she cannot go with us to some event because Elizabeth is ill, and so forth. We may find this amusing, but if Mary is insistent that this is no game, no pretense, but is quite literally true, we will be—to put it gently—skeptical. As we try to get Mary to admit that there is no real invisible elephant, we will be likely to seek ways of testing her claims. "Show us her footprints." "How does she fit through the doorways?" "Where are the leftovers from her meals?" "Why do we never hear her?" Such devices will elicit the information that Elizabeth is not only invisible, but intangible, inaudible, nonspatial, and so forth. There will turn out to be no way in which Elizabeth's reality can be tested. Surely by now our patience with Mary will be running short. Whether we suppose that she is trying to be funny, or that she is just obstinate, or that she needs to consult with a psychiatrist, we will

not be able to take her talk about Elizabeth seriously. We will be quite convinced that there is no Elizabeth. The point being made by the logical posi-
tivists, however, was not that such an untestable alleged being does not exist,
but that talk about the untestable is *meaningless*.

What, indeed, would it *mean* to talk about Elizabeth the invisible, intangible, inaudible elephant? What would it mean to speak of any utterly undetectable "being"? Certainly there are those among us who have firm
convictions about ghosts, demons, angels, and so forth. Such believers attribute various effects to the agency of these empirically unverifiable beings.
More commonly, however, persons whose cultural conditioning is that of the
"developed" nations with the long-term effects of science and education will
judge that there are mundane causes for such effects—whether they have
been discovered yet or not.

In light of such observations, the professor using the illustration raises the
question whether it makes any more sense to talk about "God" than to talk
about an undetectable elephant or such other unverifiable alleged realities as
ghosts, demons, and angels.

The story, with the questions which it raises, illustrates several points.
First, it illustrates something about the unusual character of the traditional
use of the term "God," and therewith it indicates why the story cannot properly be supposed to constitute a refutation of "God-talk." Such a supposed
refutation would be an argument by analogy (which itself would be a fallacy)
when the analogy is not apt. The point is that an elephant is a visible, tangible, audible, and so on, entity. It is a finite creature for which such claims as
invisibility are contradictory. By contrast, what is meant by the term "God"
among believers is a *transcendent* reality. That is to say, while visibility, tangi-
bility, and so forth, are part of the accepted meaning of "elephant," these
same characteristics are *excluded* from the intention of the word "God." Any
persons who suppose that our natural skepticism about an undetectable finite
entity should apply equally to affirmations concerning "God" simply do not
understand the latter term. To put it another way, such a would-be argument
against the reality or the meaningfulness of "God-talk" would be guilty of the
fallacy of begging the question. If the question is whether God is, and it is understood that God transcends the limitations and structures that characterize
finite beings (creatures), an argument which answers in the negative on the
grounds that "God" must not be because empirical tests (appeals to the evidence available to human sense perception) do not show evidence of such a
being clearly requires the *assumption* that there can be only finite and empirically testable beings. That is, it *assumes* that God cannot be; it does not offer a valid argument to that effect. If the question is whether "God-talk" is
meaningful, the logical situation is the same. There is no valid argument, because the alleged argument begins by begging the very question at issue.

This recognition that the professor's illustration does not establish the un-reality of God or the meaninglessness of religious and theological language does not mean either that there are no problems concerning "God-talk" or that the illustration is irrelevant. On the contrary, the fact that so many persons find such illustrations to be persuasive against belief in God makes an important point about modern cultures such as ours. The enormous impact of scientific developments upon these cultures has tended to make us "empiricists." How often do we say such things as "seeing is believing," or "I'm from Missouri," or simply "Show me"? In stark contrast to the peoples of the premodern eras of Christianity, we do not naturally assume that there are various sorts of invisible, intangible, causal agents at work all about us. When affirmations of such beings are made we are skeptical, and we press the makers of such affirmations for "evidence." This is our "empiricism." It should be pointed out, though, that if we assert or assume that only what can be established by natural scientific methods can be "real," we are not being scientific, but *scientistic*. The latter term indicates that one has leapt from the realm of science to that of metaphysics, elevating the methods appropriate to the limited ranges of scientific investigation beyond those limits into a sup-posed basis for making judgments about ultimate reality. That this is a fallacy does not, however, deny the importance in theology of recognizing this common characteristic of persons today that makes it so difficult to convey theology's intended meanings.

The professor's illustration also, however, underlines the fact that the difficulty of conveying theology's intended meanings is not just or even primarily due to the empiricism of modern persons. It is due, rather, to the in-commensurability of human language and deity. The very effort to explain the question-begging character of any positivistic argument against the meaningfulness of religious and theological language manifests the inherent difficulty of attempts to employ human language in description of the reality intended in such language. Language is finite, historically and culturally relative, and in most of its uses it is inescapably ambiguous. What are we to say of the "subject" of religious and theological language?

When we say that faith's God-talk intends a reality beyond the limits and structures of finite beings, that God is the transcendent, holy, spiritual Creator of all else that is, we not only employ terms that are most difficult to clarify, but we find ourselves entangled in logical difficulties. Whatever we say is questionable. If we say that we are referring to "a reality that . . . ," the expression ("a reality") suggests that we are speaking of something that is a member of a class. That would imply that it is less than the structures which establish that class of "realities." That, however, is contrary to the intentions of the statement. It could only be a finite being, something which is limited, bound, less than ultimate, not Creator, not utterly trustworthy. It is easy to

see why some concluded long ago that theology should employ only a "negative way."

It is also easy to see why scholars in an empirically minded culture would
propose that "meaning is verifiability." Much difficulty was experienced by
those scholars, however, in their efforts to find an adequate formulation of
that basic definition of meaning. The problem was that if the definition were
strict enough to exclude metaphysics, ethics, and theology from "meaningfulness," it also excluded important scientific statements. Natural science
proceeds in part by the formulation of imaginative hypotheses. In many
cases, when these hypotheses are first developed no one can yet see how they
can be tested. Since natural science was the model of meaning, such observations indicated the untenability of the narrower forms of the idea that "meaning is verifiability." Interpretations broad enough to include such hypotheses
no longer excluded the kinds of discourse that these scholars were convinced
were meaningless.

Further, some critics argued that the doctrine that only empirically verifiable statements are meaningful must itself be meaningless because it is
not subject to empirical verification. In response, some argued that it was
a tautology, that is, that the definition of meaning in terms of empirical
verifiability was simply a clarification of what is intended by the word
"meaning." Others contended that the statement *is* empirically verifiable,
that "in fact" only empirically verifiable statements are meaningful. However, as various observers—both proponents and opponents of logical empiricism—noted, there are other meaningful uses of language besides stating
empirical matters of fact or merely giving expression to feeling. That is, "in
fact" there are clearly meaningful uses of language that are not subject to empirical verification.

Functional Analysis of Religious Language

In the course of time most of the linguistic analysts moved away from
the narrowness of "verificational analysis" to "functional analysis" of language. Rather than beginning with the dogmatic assertion that the only
meaningful discourse is that which asserts matters of fact (as is implied in the
verification principle), they sought to examine various kinds of discourse
and discover how they functioned and thus what kind of meaning they have.
One may note that this is a much more empirical approach. Its proponents
pointed out that we use language meaningfully to ask questions, to give or-
ders, and even to effect changes. This last use has been called "performa-
tive." Examples would include such statements as the following (when they
are employed in the appropriate circumstances by authorized persons): "I
now pronounce that you are husband and wife . . ."; "I bequeath all of my
worldly goods to . . ."; "I now declare this bridge open to . . ."; "I declare

that this nation is now at war with . . . ." Certainly such statements will ordinarily have effects that are empirically verifiable, but that is not what constitutes their "meaning." Their meaning is not in describing a state of affairs, but in changing or creating it.

Linguistic analysts and theologians employing the methods of functional analysis have proposed several understandings of the meaning of religious (and theological) language. R. B. Braithwaite (b. 1900), for example, who agrees that meaning is to be found in the *use* rather than the verifiability of statements, but who shares the logical empiricists' insistence that the meaning "be tied to empirical use" (Braithwaite 1955, 33), contends that the primary meaning of religious statements is to express intentions to act in certain ways. "I myself take the typical meaning of the body of Christian assertions as being given by their proclaiming intentions to follow an agapeistic way of life, and for a description of this way of life—a description in general and metaphorical terms, but an empirical description nonetheless—I should quote most of the Thirteenth Chapter of I Corinthians" (ibid., 19). Even when they manifest commitments to the same modes of conduct, religions differ from one another in the *stories* the adherents of the particular religions associate with their commitments. These stories, he says, serve a psychological function, aiding one in willing to follow the indicated intentions, but those followers need not believe those stories to be factually true. "In religious conviction the resolution to follow a way of life is primary; it is not derived from believing, still less from thinking of any empirical story. The story may psychologically support the resolution, but it does not logically justify it" (ibid., 31).

As critics have pointed out, this way of accounting for the meaning intended in the use of religious language is clearly not in accordance with the understanding of most serious users of such language, whether they be theologically educated or not. The positivist spirit is still present, and the religious spirit is not. It is an outsider's description, and therein it lacks one of the usual tenets of "functional analysis"—that it is the users themselves who must indicate how their assertions "mean."

A much less reductive attempt to use functional linguistic analysis to clarify the meaning of religious language for an empirically minded society is to be found in Ian T. Ramsey's *Religious Language: An Empirical Placing of Theological Phrases*, first published in 1957. Rather than asking directly what kind of meaning religious language has, Ramsey poses two questions: (1) "To what kind of situation does religion appeal?" (2) "For these situations, what language is appropriate currency?" His answer to the first question is that a genuinely religious situation involves "an odd discernment" and "a total commitment." "Odd" here is not a derogatory term. Its intention is to affirm that what one "sees" is different from empirical matters and, indeed, from all everyday experience (other than the religious). That "oddness" is implied in the suggestion of "total" commitment being appropriate to it. "Total" indicates that it has to do with the whole business of life, that one's life is understood and lived in terms of it, even that one's life could be given for it. The two factors are mutually entailing. The religious discernment without total commitment would be hypocrisy. The total commitment without the (odd) religious discernment would be bigotry and idolatry (Ramsey 1957, 18). The religious situation, then, is not a matter of facts that can be observed with detachment, but one of involvement, total personal involvement. "So we see religious commitment as a *total* commitment to the *whole* universe; something in relation to which argument has only a very odd function; its purpose being to tell such a tale as evokes the 'insight,' the 'discernment' from which the commitment follows as a response" (ibid., 37).

Because the religious situation is "odd," so also is religious language. It uses "object language," but it uses it in strangely qualified ways. For example, Christian language speaks of "creation *ex nihilo*," of "eternal life," and of "the Fall of man." In each of the former two phrases there is a logical impropriety. The first seems to suggest that "nothing" (*nihilo*) is that from which something is made. The second describes "life" as transcending time, when our experience of life is that it is pervasively and inescapably temporal. In each of these cases there is a familiar noun that is modified by an adjective or phrase which is not appropriate to the ordinary meaning of the noun. In the language of the linguistic analysts, we are dealing here with "models" and "qualifiers." The term "model" indicates that the noun is not being used in its common, everyday sense. The "qualifier" shows this by the very fact that it does not "fit" with that noun when it is used in its usual ways.

In the third case, "the Fall of man," there is a phrase which sounds like others such as "the fall of the Roman Empire" or "the fall of King Louis." In those cases, however, something that has specifiable empirical meaning is referred to as having fallen. (Even in these cases the use of the term "fall" is metaphorical rather than literal.) But what does it mean to speak of "the Fall of man"? We know that it intends the whole of humankind, but what, then, is meant by "Fall"? Those who are familiar with Christian tradition will be tempted to offer orthodox answers, but that is not the point. The point is to note that those answers are in reference to something quite unlike ordinary experience. Ramsey, using the suggestions of the linguistic analysts, points out that the oddness (as compared with ordinary empirical references) and the use of the capital letter "F" in "Fall" signal the reader or the hearer that this is a special use of language appealing to an odd situation. The logical impropriety in the phrases is not an indication of carelessness or stupidity. It is, rather, an intended sign of the difference of meaning in religious language as compared with conventional discourse. "Indeed, the curse of much theological apologetic is that it talks as if theological language worked like ordinary matter-of-fact language, which is precisely what his opponents wish to hear the theologian say, for then theology has lost the day before the battle begins" (ibid., 82). Rather is it the case that religious meaning is that which is only grasped when there is that unusual discernment that evokes total commitment, meaning that will not be grasped correctly in detachment, but only in deep personal involvement.

Religious language then, as compared with conventional discourse, is always odd. It is "object language and more," pointing beyond the spatiotemporal and the conventional by use of special qualifications and logical improprieties, by the use of technical terms, by typographical devices, and by mixing universes of discourse (ibid., 39–40). The last may be seen in such phrases as "the Lord is my shepherd," and "I am the vine."

Being "odd" is not all that must be said to characterize religious language, however, for there are other kinds of discourse that are also odd and to be distinguished from object language. Another important characteristic of religious language, according to Ramsey, is its use of "significant tautologies." The purpose of these tautologies is to draw attention to key words that indicate "ultimates of explanation" (ibid., 40). It is the character of religious phrases as involving total commitment that entails the need for these ultimates of explanation. Ramsey suggests an analogy with some expressions in the language or moral commitment. There are some persons whose sense of duty is such that to ask them why they do their duty can only be answered by some such phrase as "duty is duty." Rather than meaningless, the statement indicates a complete commitment. To ask for some further explanation is simply to show the failure to understand that kind of moral commitment. Ramsey proposes that all one can do is tell the sort of stories that may evoke the discernment of such morality.

As an example of a significant tautology in Christian language, Ramsey discusses the affirmation that "God is love." He notes that this is not the same as the statement that "God is loving." That would be a familiar everyday kind of statement. But to say "God is love" is not. We have heard it so often, however, that we fail to see its logical oddness. Ramsey sees it as a tautology, a statement that repeats in the predicate what is present in the subject, like "duty is duty" or "a rose is a rose." A theological tautology is not meaningless, however, for the purpose of the tautology is to indicate the ultimacy ascribed to the term "God," a "key" term for Christian religious discourse. The point is essentially the same as noting that one who asks "Where did God come from?" or "Who was God's father?" simply does not understand the term "God." One might answer, "God is God." The tautology sounds meaningless, but it indicates the inappropriateness of the questions. To some it will sound like the parent who says with exasperation, "Because I said so!" or "Because I told you to!" In these cases, one recognizes an unreasonable arbitrariness. The parent is finite and fallible, so the appeal to ultimate authority does not ring true. Instead it reveals the finitude and the fallibility. Those for whom the religious tautologies sound like unreasonable arbitrariness do not share the discernment/commitment of the sincere users of Christian religious language, and accordingly, they do not understand their affirmations. The religious spokespersons cannot remove the misunderstanding by entering wholly into the object language of the nonbelievers, however, for this would surrender the very possibility of indicating the ultimacy of their commitment. They can but seek ways to evoke the odd discernment and the total commitment that it entails, and the language they employ will necessarily be "odd."

In order to develop and illustrate the importance of recognizing the oddness of Christian religious discourse, Ramsey discusses many biblical and traditional Christian phrases. Among these are virgin birth, crucifixion, resurrection, and ascension. Three of these have what is traditionally seen as a "miraculous" character. The fourth, however, the crucifixion, seems to be a quite straightforward empirical event. The crucifixion of Jesus of Nazareth could have been described in vivid accurate detail by any careful observer, and its factual character thereby have become known to any attentive listener. Thus far, however, we do not deal with Christian religious language. The factual crucifixion of Jesus of Nazareth does not have the religious meaning of the Christian affirmation of the crucifixion of Jesus Christ. Ramsey draws attention to the contexts within which the crucifixion is affirmed in Scripture and in the Creeds. For example, the Nicene Creed puts the affirmation within the context of a "for us," which makes a great deal of difference as to the meaning of the affirmation. According to the accounts, there were three crucifixions in that place that day and three crosses, but Christians speak of "the crucifixion" and of "the cross." Here, as well as in affirmations of virgin birth, resurrection, and ascension, the *meaning* of the Christian religious affirmation is not reducible to the "facts." In every case the meaning is rooted in the affirmation of "what God was and is doing" "for us and for our salvation." The oddness is indicated in many ways. Arguments about the "facts" are beside the point. Without the odd discernment evoking the total commitment, the meaning is missed. Unfortunately, many Christians labor under the assumption that "faith" consists in believing incredible "facts." Many non-Christians have the same misunderstanding: they do not hear the oddness of the language of Christian tradition, and turn away from what, to them, is credulity and irrationality.

Participationists versus Rationalists

The efforts of Ramsey and others to find help in the techniques of linguistic analysis for the task of overcoming such misunderstandings in societies deeply influenced by the empirical methods of modern science make primary use of the discriminations of logic, the science that seeks to clarify the laws of sound reasoning. Other Christian scholars, whose numbers have been growing considerably of late, focus their attention upon the discernments of literary criticism and the techniques of literature. Though this focus is different, there need not be any conflict with an approach such as Ramsey's.

Ramsey speaks at several points of the need to tell stories in order to evoke the odd discernment/total commitment. Many Christian interpreters today believe that this appeal to story (or to narrative, including metaphor, allegory, parable, etc.) is the crucial insight for understanding Christian religious language and for reformulating Christian theology.

What kind (or kinds) of language use is (or are) best suited to proclaiming the gospel and making known the grace of God? An effort like Ramsey's to "place" religious and theological language *empirically* is very restricting. Even so, Ramsey has presented a case for the judgment that careful attention to the "logic" of religious language reveals that its use includes pointing *beyond* the observable (the empirically verifiable), that its reference is "deeper" and more inclusive, and that it seeks to evoke a *participation*. Religious language, in this view, is not objective reference or neutral description. Facts are relevant, but they do not constitute the full or basic subject matter. That which the key words such as "God" intend is never an object and is not comprehensible without changes in persons—as distinguished from changes only in their ideas.

It should be noted that there is no more agreement here than on most other issues in contemporary theology. On these questions of language and meaning there is a continuum of viewpoints extending from the thoroughly rationalistic (for which a changing of ideas *is* the essential change in persons) to the thoroughly "participationist" for which the points of the previous paragraph are fine—as far as they go. For the sake of greater clarity, this discussion will set these two extremes over against each other, but it should be remembered that a considerable variety of positions lies between the two extremes.

The disagreements involve much more than judgments about the uses of language. Essentially entailed (and interdependent) are one's understanding of *God*, of *human being*, of *faith*, and therefore one's understanding of theological *meaning* and of religious *truth*. In a modern Western culture the more rationalistic understandings of each of these subjects are the ones likely to be taken for granted. For that reason, the following exposition will focus on the less familiar "participationist" orientation.

Parabolic Meaning

The difference can be seen in the treatment of parables. Throughout much of Christian history, the parables have been interpreted as allegories. An allegory is a literary device (though it can also be dramatic or pictorial) in which there is a second and hidden meaning beneath the surface depiction. An example may be seen in the seventeenth chapter of Ezekiel in which a story about two great eagles is told in verses 3–10 and then explained in verses 11–21 showing that each element in the story stands for something else. The eagles, for example, represent the king of Babylon and the pharaoh of Egypt. The story serves to get attention and to illustrate a point. That point or meaning, however, can be said directly and clearly. The interpretation states clearly what is hidden in the allegory itself. The direct statement displaces the story.

In the fourth chapter of the Gospel according to Mark, Jesus' tale of the Sower is treated in just this fashion, that is, as an allegory. In the tenth verse, following the report of Jesus' words to the crowd, the text continues, "And when he was alone, those who were about him with the twelve asked him concerning the parables. And he said to them, 'To you has been given the secret of the kingdom of God, but for those outside everything is in parables; so that they may indeed see but not perceive, and may indeed hear but not understand; lest they should turn again, and be forgiven.' And he said to them, 'Do you not understand this parable? How then will you understand all the parables? The sower sows the word . . .'" (Mark 4:10–14). And the explanation continues, stating directly the hidden meanings of the several elements of the tale. Thus, here and elsewhere, Mark interprets the parables as allegories, reporting, indeed, that this was Jesus' own explanation of their nature and purpose.

It is hardly surprising, then, that before the impact of historical-critical biblical scholarship the parables of Jesus were commonly treated as allegories. Modern scholarship gradually led, however, to the conviction that such interpretations as this one in Mark 4:10–20 were not a part of Jesus' teaching, but represented the understanding of the Evangelists. One will naturally ask, if the allegorical interpretations given in Mark, Matthew, and Luke were not part of Jesus' teaching, what was (is) the meaning of the parable? But this way of putting the question fails to take account of an important point that is very much a matter of disagreement. The question seems to ask for an interpretive statement of the ideas the parable is presumed to represent indirectly. A doctrinal (or moral) proposition is assumed to be the *real* meaning of the parable. This is the rationalistic position, for which direct statements of ideas to be grasped by the intellect are the best vehicle for meaning and truth, and for which figurative modes of expression, while they may serve to gain attention, aid memory, and illustrate ideas, are less clear, ambiguous, and best replaced by direct statements. By contrast, biblical scholars who have immersed themselves in literature and literary criticism have come increasingly to the conclusion that such rationalism fundamentally misunderstands the parables (and many other literary forms employed in Scripture and Christian tradition).

For these scholars, the meaning of a parable is to be found *in* the parable, and it cannot be stated more adequately or even adequately in nonfigurative propositions. Instead of asking "What does the parable mean?" one must first ask "*How* does the parable mean?"

In order to answer this question, it is necessary to be more specific about the use of the term "parable" than tradition has been, for not only in other literature, but also in the New Testament reports of Jesus' teaching, there is a wide variety of figurative modes of speech that have all been called parables. These include "example stories" and "similitudes" as well as parables in the stricter sense. J. D. Crossan distinguishes between uses of figurative language which "move toward . . . illustrating information on their referent (examples, allegories)" and those which move toward "creating participation in their referent (metaphors, symbols) . . ." (Crossan 1973, 21).

The key to note here is the contrast of "illustrating information" and "creating participation." "Creating participation" is an aspect of the way in which Crossan and various other scholars use the terms "metaphor" and "symbol," terms which are, however, used by many others much more broadly. The term "symbol" is commonly used to refer to anything that "stands for" something else. Hence, one often hears statements about that which is "merely symbolic," the implication being that the meaning (or the degree of reality) is superficial, usually as compared with the literal. As Crossan (and others such as Paul Tillich and C. G. Jung) uses the word "symbol," however, it is contradictory to say "merely symbolic," for by "symbol" they intend something that has deep communicative power, which, indeed, evokes *participation* in the intended meaning. They use the word "sign" for the kind of "standing for" that is superficial and impacts only upon intellect. In like fashion, Crossan distinguishes metaphor from other figures of speech, not by the presence or absence of terms indicating comparison ("like" or "as"), but by the effect or impact of the locution. To the extent that the only result is an intellectual recognition of a comparison and not also an involvement of imagination, feeling, will, indeed of the self, the figurative language has fallen short of metaphoric meaning. "A true metaphor is one whose power creates the participation whereby its truth is experienced" (ibid., 18). Amos N. Wilder has expressed the point in similar terms. "Now we know that a true metaphor or symbol is more than a sign, it is a bearer of the reality to which it refers. The hearer not only learns about the reality, he participates in it. He is invaded by it. . . . Jesus' speech had the character not of instruction and of ideas but of compelling imagination, of spell, of mythical shock and transformation" (Wilder 1971, 84).

· Parable, then, for scholars like Crossan and Wilder, is metaphoric and symbolic. Metaphor is verbal symbol, and parable is extended poetic metaphor. The power they see in Jesus' parables is not simply or primarily in their illustrating Jesus' *ideas* concerning God (though they may also do that), but in their communicating Jesus' *experience* of God (Crossan 1973, 22). It would, of course, be claiming too much to suggest that the hearers of Jesus' parables thereby also shared Jesus' experience of God—unless something much more than the literal is understood by "hearers." It can, however, be said that the parables confronted their hearers with a challenge to risk faith in the God experienced by Jesus.

Disagreements regarding the nature and meaning of Jesus' story of the Good Samaritan may help to illustrate this distinction. Many prominent New Testament interpreters have judged that this story is not a parable in the stricter sense of that term, but an "exemplary story." Thus it presents an example of neighborliness, showing the hearers what they should do. It calls for involvement, for full response to the needs before us even at personal sacrifice and risk, and in repudiation of our human distinctions regarding who is worthy, and so forth. Insofar as such interpretations offer prose teachings that are believed to state more clearly what the story only illustrates, these interpretations deny that the story is a parable—in the sense indicated above —and/or deny the participationist view of religious truth and meaning.

After a brief summary of several such interpretations of Jesus' story, Crossan argues that these interpreters have been misled by the context given in Luke, and that the story in its earlier form was a parable in the stricter sense (ibid., 57–66). For present purposes most of the reasons given for this judgment can be omitted. One of those reasons is important here, however, insofar as it bears directly on what it means to see the story as a parable and not just as an example. It is the point concerning Jesus' selection of a Samaritan. Crossan argues that if Jesus had been concerned only to illustrate the kind of conduct that obedience to the will of God entails, it would hardly have been helpful for this Jewish teacher instructing a Jewish audience in a Jewish setting to have introduced such a despised enemy in this central role in the story. It intrudes and interferes with such a point. Indeed, the hearers may well have been expecting that, after the description of the priest and the Levite, the third and rightly acting person would be a Jewish layperson. If the purpose is to illustrate that for God there are no bounds to the love to be shown to neighbors, it would have served well to have the beaten victim be an outcast, even a Samaritan. But no, the Samaritan is the "good" one here, and that had to be a shocking violation of possible perceptions for a Jewish audience of that time. It is hard for us today to gain any serious sense of that shock, even though New Testament specialists inform us that the alienation of Jews and Samaritans was so great that a pious Jew of that time would probably rather have died than be ministered to by a Samaritan.

Crossan argues that as a parable, and not merely an example, Jesus' story has both the literal point—that the action of the Samaritan is to be imitated —*and* a metaphorical point.

> The metaphorical point is that *just so* does the Kingdom of God break abruptly into human consciousness and demand the overturn of prior values, closed options, set judgments, and established conclusions. But the full force of the parabolic challenge is that the *just so* of the metaphorical level is not ontologically distinct from the presence of the literal point. The hearer struggling with the contradictory dualism of Good/Samaritan is actually experiencing in and through this the inbreaking of the Kingdom. Not only does it happen like this, it happens in this. (Ibid., 65–66)

Thus, while one can offer a statement of the parable's meaning, that statement is not its meaning. The meaning must be lived or participated in. One "understands" God's kingdom by letting go of self-protective devices such as believing that one is among the good people and "they" (Samaritans!) are the bad ones.

Robert Funk puts essentially the same understanding of the parable of the Good Samaritan somewhat more graphically. Funk describes Jesus' drawing of his listeners into his story, for example, by evoking their natural agreement with the anticlericalism expressed in the passing by of the priest and the Levite. Jesus entered into his hearers' "language world," but then broke that world open on "the rock of grace." Here it is the shock of the naming of a Samaritan where the engaged listener is expecting a humble layperson like him- or herself. ". . . The narrative is not complete until the hearer is drawn into it as participant, the hearer is confronted with a situation in relation to which he must decide how to comport himself: is he willing to allow himself to be the victim, to smile at the affront to the priest and Levite, to be served by an enemy? The parable invites, nay, compels him to make some response. And it is this response that is decisive for him" (Funk 1966, 214).

D. O. Via, Jr., though disagreeing about the classification of the Good Samaritan as parable in the stricter sense, nevertheless agrees with Crossan and Funk about the nature and primacy of parabolic meaning. The intention, he argues, of both the parable and its interpretation is to "involve the hearer in the subject matter," to inject "a new possibility into the situation of [the] hearers," to bring about a changed situation in the hearers' lives (Via 1967, 53). Via goes on to quote with approval the position of Ian Crombie that theological statements are given content and related to experience by their being treated as parables. If, for example, we make an affirmation of the love of God, ". . . we do not know literally what love is in the being of God, but we trust that a parable like The Prodigal Son puts us sufficiently in touch with God to enter into relations with him which bring about our ultimate well-being" (ibid., 64). It is in participating in the world embodied in the parable that we "know" God's love.

One may appropriately ask whether this discussion has not passed over the disagreement about the classification of the story of the Good Samaritan too hastily. If it does not matter whether it is a parable or not, why so much fuss about parables? By way of response from the viewpoint insisting on the primacy of parabolic meaning, one might argue that even if the story of the Good Samaritan is judged to be an example whose immediate point might be stated in the admonition to act as the Samaritan acted, Jesus' parabolic language world is not escaped. For Christians, as for the original hearers, it is important that Jesus is the storyteller, for in addition to embodying the truth of God's kingdom in his parables, Jesus embodied (incarnated) that living truth in his life. Jesus used many forms of language in his teachings, and these teachings as a whole (together with his life and ministry as a whole) constitute parabolic truth. That context would hardly be irrelevant to such an "example" as Jesus' story of the Good Samaritan. Even taken simply as an example, the story leaves the hearers with a moral demand that they are unable in themselves to obey. Can I simply choose to be free of my most passionate prejudices and to give generously of myself and my resources to persons whom I have despised? Hardly. The challenge to take the risk of trusting wholly in the grace of God is still present. The meaning is still participative.

Narrative Theology

The specific focus upon parable as the most appropriate linguistic vehicle for theological meaning is representative of only a small part of the contemporary theological spectrum, but what has been said of it is generally applicable to the larger movement that emphasizes the category of *narrative*. Parable is but one of many forms of narrative. Allegory, fable, myth, drama, short story, and novel are included here, but so also are biography, autobiography, and history. The last, history, may surprise some at first, but a little reflection reminds one that history is never a mere factual report of "what happened." Every telling of history involves selection, first of all because far too much "happens" during a single day of even one life to allow the possibility of its all being reported in all of its details, and such events in one life are not fully reported apart from their entanglements with other lives, with society, culture, and so forth. The historian's selection of events and of factors contributing to those events involves a point of view that guides an interpretation. The interpretation governs the historian's *plotting* of the narrative of the chosen segment of history. The verb "governs" here is not intended to suggest a lack of concern for accuracy and honesty on the part of the historian, but only to indicate the inescapable intrusion of the historian into the "reporting." History is necessarily a form of narrative that, in degree, shares basic characteristics of fictional stories.

Given such an understanding, it is evident that a very large part of the Jewish and Christian Scriptures is made up of narratives. The recognition of this fact has its own importance in the interpretation of those documents, but it is not yet the point of narrative theology. Academic theology, as it has developed over the centuries of Christian history, has not usually had a clear and direct narrative form. Much more of narrative is evident in the liturgies, hymns, dramas, and preaching of Christian history. Is this important for academic theology? Should it have a direct or indirect narrative character? An increasing number of contemporary theologians are urging an affirmative answer.

Michael Goldberg, a rabbi and Jewish theologian, has examined a wide variety of current proposals for narrative theology in his book *Theology and Narrative: A Critical Introduction.* In the midst of their differences, he is able to indicate several points of essential common ground. Such theologies, he finds, affirm the primacy of narrative. The narratives they commend, unlike fables, are not simply engaging and illustrative ways of expressing meanings and truths that can be better stated in propositions, doctrines, and laws. Rather, the meaning and truth are *in* the narratives. This is because human lives and human experience have themselves a narrative character. Further, persons need "stories" that give shape and meaning to their lives within which they can make some sense of the joys, trials, and traumas of their existence. Doctrines and laws do not fulfill this purpose, though they may serve to support and interpret the stories in and by which persons live—provided that they do not replace those stories. The reason, again, is that, according to these perspectives, human life and experience and therefore reality itself—as we participate in it—have the character of narrative.

Because human lives have a narrative character, narratives have a capacity to engage hearers, to evoke participation in the story being told, to challenge the lives and stories of the hearers, and, sometimes, to precipitate a transformation in those lives. This is central to the power of biography and autobiography. The narrative of another's life can challenge one's narrative understanding of his or her own life. But this is true also of novels, if they "ring true" to the experience of the readers. Such challenge need not occur, however, and the narratives, whether fictional or (insofar as possible) nonfictional, may serve only for escape, or they may be boringly irrelevant. Another reason why the challenge does not occur is that the appropriate stories are not being told. Goldberg quotes Carol P. Christ's argument:

> Women's stories have not been told. And without stories there is no articulation of experience. . . . Without stories [a woman] cannot understand herself. Without stories she is alienated from those deeper experiences of self and world that have been called spiritual or religious. . . . The expression of women's spiritual quest is integrally related to the telling of women's stories. If women's stories are not told, the depth of women's souls will not be known. (Quoted in Goldberg 1981, 12–13)

If it is true that human lives have the character of narrative, that the human mind works narratively, that persons find meaning for their lives and experience reality in terms of narratives, that narratives have affective and transformative power for us, and that meaning and truth are therefore *in* the narratives which accordingly are not merely preliminary to interpretive propositions stating "the real truth," what does this imply for theology?

Even if all of the foregoing claims were agreed upon, there would yet be room for disagreement on this question, and such disagreement is indeed to be found today. It can be argued that theology itself should be in narrative forms. Certainly it is possible to judge that poets (employing symbol, metaphor, parable, etc.), novelists, and other narrators have done and do more to confront our lives with the challenge and possibility of faith, of new life and meaning, than propositionally oriented academic theologians have done or are doing. Such an argument will require attention, however, to disagreements about the nature of human being, of faith, and of truth. These questions are indeed at the heart of the whole discussion of language, meaning, and truth in theology.

In various periods of the history of Christian doctrine and perhaps more so today, the tendency has been to see the essence of human being in the capacity for conscious reasoning. This is surely *an* essential human characteristic, one without which human existence as we know it would be quite impossible. If conscious reasoning is the central defining aspect of human being, it follows that *faith* is essentially a rational commitment to doctrinally formulated beliefs. The "right" doctrines will be understood to be a correct statement of the *truth*, "truth" being interpreted as a correspondence between the rationally grasped doctrines and the realities themselves. Such rationalism, while it is commonly associated with the modern "liberalisms" produced by the successes of modern science and technology and their need for objective clarity, is, interestingly, present also in many forms of religious conservatism as reflected in their identification of the truth with a particular set of doctrines and of faith with belief in those doctrines. The difference, usually, is that the "liberals" are more concerned that the belief be accompanied by understanding and that the doctrines correspond with the whole range of human experience. The "liberal" viewpoints being generally described here not only see human being, faith, and truth in terms of conscious reason, but, unlike some very conservative positions, they grant to reason a major status as authority in theology.

Important as these differences between rationalistic liberals and rationalistic conservatives are, both views reject the arguments of the narrativists as noted above. For the rationalistically inclined, the meaning and truth will be far more in the doctrines than in the narratives. Persons will be understood to change their lives by reasoned perception and rationally guided choice, and the seductions of narratives will be critically guarded against. There may well be a place for narratives, for songs, and for rituals, but those vehicles will be secondary and subservient to proper theological language.

In response to the appeal of the narrativists to the preponderance of narrative texts in the Scriptures, defenders of the primacy of doctrinal interpretations can appeal to the historical importance of New Testament letters, especially those of Paul, arguing that it is here that Christian theology proper had its beginnings. These documents do indeed seem to make their appeals to conscious reasoning as the locus of appropriate understanding and not to employ narrative or other participationist strategies in doing so. This is, however, by no means an undisputed judgment. Robert Funk, for example, has interpreted Paul's letters as employing the same essential strategy as the parables, entering into the language world of the intended hearers in order to break those closed worlds open on the rock of grace (Funk 1966, 224–305). Hans Dieter Betz, in his *Galatians: A Commentary on Paul's Letter to the Churches in Galatia*, has sought to show the importance of recognizing that Paul was here employing the rhetorical and literary techniques and forms of his culture (Betz 1979). Norman R. Petersen has more specifically insisted upon the narrative characteristics of Paul's letters in his *Rediscovering Paul: Philemon and the Sociology of Paul's Narrative World*. As the title suggests, Petersen particularly emphasizes the importance of recognizing the "narrative world" of Paul's letters. He also seeks to demonstrate the presence of such narrative characteristics as "plotting." All such approaches are innovative and controversial, but they show the basic questions to be open. The position of narrative theologians does not stand or fall with this question about the narrative or nonnarrative character of Paul's letters, though the acknowledged importance of those writings in the history of Christian theology does make their example important in the discussions of the relations between narrative and theology.

It is possible, of course, to have any of a number of viewpoints which lie between the more extreme rationalist and the more extreme "participationist" views of truth and meaning, but questions concerning whether the priority of meaning lies with the narrative linguistic forms or with the propositional-doctrinal forms will remain crucial. This difference and its importance can be seen in connection with both sacrament and sermon. What purpose is served by the Eucharist? In an earlier time most Christians might have been expected to see that purpose as the miraculous communication of grace, when by "miraculous" was meant a supernatural causal intervention by God. With the eclipse of supernaturalism in the modern era, some persons have been inclined to view this sacrament as no more than a device for reminding us of past events whose meaning can be stated fully and clearly in theological propositions. On that basis, if we, the congregation, would listen carefully, a short lecture would really be more useful than would carrying out the ritual. By contrast, if the purpose of the sacrament is to evoke a greater awareness of and openness to the gracious presence of God as that was embodied in the life and death of Jesus Christ and is now "known" by participation in a personal relationship (faith), then telling the story and enacting participation in it with the aid of symbols and poetic-symbolic words will be immeasurably more meaningful than a lecture. It would be possible to go too far in either direction, for ritual practices wholly unrelated to instruction and critical reflection might well have only emotional and superstitious effects.

In the case of preaching, which is more similar to theology than is ritual practice insofar as both are verbal, all those who have been exposed to very many sermons are aware that there is great variety in the practice. What kind of communication is intended, what result is sought? For purposes of the present analogy, and leaving aside those sermons one may discern to be intended primarily to impress the congregation with the preacher, let us assume that the sermons to be compared seek to be founded upon a scriptural source for their message. Even with such a common basis, some sermons leave the biblical source buried under the preacher's interpretation, evidently intending to leave the congregation with a memory of the preacher's theological and/or ethical instructions. Other sermons, however, exposit the scriptural source(s) in such a way as to bring the listeners more into touch with that more original witness in its relevance to those listeners' lives. One might say that the preacher and the sermon get out of the way of the biblical witness and leave the congregation challenged in their lives by the biblical story rather than confronted merely by information or instruction. The latter approach would, in other words, be intended to facilitate the taking of the risk of faith (understood relationally, not rationalistically), and not only to add to a stock of ideas or, perhaps, to change those ideas.

What of theology, then, if the judgments of the narrative theologians are accepted? While it might be argued that theology should take an entirely narrative form itself, this is not usually what is commended. Rather, academic theology is seen as properly taking a role like the second form of preaching or of the sort of instruction that would protect the sacraments from merely emotional and supernaturalistic employments. To put it in another way, theology is seen in rough analogy to the work of literary critics, in which the critics do not seek by their interpretations to displace literary works with clearer statements of what the poems, dramas, novels, and the like, "say," but to facilitate the possibilities of the literary works' communicating their own aesthetically embodied meanings. The role of academic theology for a narrativist would then be that of *a secondary language* of the church employed in reflection upon the primary languages, those of directly narrative character of one sort or another.

Theology of the Imagination, Symbolic
Theology, and Theopoetic

This judgment that the language of academic theology is not the primary language of Christian faith, that it does not provide the most direct expression of Christian experience and conviction, is not held only by proponents of narrative theology. Just as "narrative theology" is a more inclusive concept than "parabolic theology," so also may "narrative theology" be seen as finding its place in more inclusive understandings of participationist religious meaning suggested by such terms as "symbolic theology," "theology of the imagination," and theology as "theopoetic."

Amos Wilder is but one of many contemporary theologians who have argued that far-greater attention is needed to the role of imagination. He shares the judgment that religious language in general has suffered from a captivity to rationalistic prejudice and its preference for discursive and prosaic modes of expression.

My plea for a theopoetic means doing more justice to the role of the symbolic and the prerational in the way we deal with experience. We should recognize that human nature and human societies are more deeply motivated by images and fabulations than by ideas. This is where power lies and the future is shaped.

This plea therefore means according a greater role to the imagination in all aspects of the religious life. But "imagination" here should not be taken in an insipid sense. Imagination is a necessary component of all profound knowing and celebration; all remembering, realizing, and anticipating; all faith, hope, and love. When imagination fails doctrines become ossified, witness and proclamation wooden, doxologies and litanies empty, consolations hollow, and ethics legalistic. (Wilder 1976, 2)

Here again the emphasis is upon the understanding of human being, experiencing, meaning, and becoming, and the contrast with those who understand human beings rationalistically is clear. This, however, is not the full basis for proposing that the poetic-symbolic vision of divinity, theopoesis, is more fundamental than theology in its more usual discursive forms. It is also because of the character of divinity, its glory and its mystery (ibid., 12).

It is because they judge that the human spirit is much more than intellect and that persons experience meaning multidimensionally, and also because deity is for us the mystery of holy grace to which humans are more deeply opened by symbol, myth, and metaphor, that those we are calling "participationists" also insist upon a need to reject the narrow understandings of *truth* that hold sway in modern Western cultures. It is indeed very hard for us to escape the conviction that "the true" is "the factual." One may recall the energies that have been spent in the past in the effort to discover what kind of "great fish" is most likely to have been able to swallow Jonah whole and contain him alive for his famous journey, and, on the other hand, the many persons who have concluded that the story of Jonah is meaningless if or because it is not historical fact, that is, if it is not "true." But that story may be seen to portray and embody much more truth about God and persons, indeed, religious persons, than a merely factual report of past events.

Similarly, the author of Job was a poet and dramatist, not a repeater of facts. That his story does not report history—in the conventional senses—does not render his work either false or meaningless. On the contrary, he offers his readers—theopoetically—a far deeper encounter with the truth of self, world, and God than most of us are willing to hear.

Some of the participationist theologians have found help in the philosopher Martin Heidegger's discussions concerning truth. To state a difficult matter oversimply, Heidegger taught that truth has the character of an event in which "unconcealment" occurs. It is an event of revelation in which, however, Holy Being, which comes to presence, remains mysterious. Truth, indeed, is described as having the character of grace. Heidegger avoided the contemporary word for grace and employed an earlier and largely forgotten German term (*Huld*), because of his conviction that our modern languages are a principal instrument of our captivity to a nonparticipative assumption concerning being, meaning, and truth. His interpretation of truth as the event of the revealing/reconcealing of Holy Being, of the coming to presence of the gracious mystery, has, of course, been subject to much criticism. Interestingly, most of these criticisms beg the question by presupposing the very understandings of truth Heidegger was seeking to overcome. Ernst Tugendhat, the author of the most thorough study of Heidegger's teachings concerning truth (Tugendhat 1967), protested (in conversation) that if Heidegger's meaning is so different from our usual uses of the term "truth," he should not have used that word but some other. As Heidegger recognized, however, if the conventional understandings of that term are allowed to stand, the battle is lost. "Truth" is an ultimate for us. So great is the power of language. Unless one is willing to leave human understandings of reality limited by what the human mind can define, thus eliminating mystery, holiness, grace, and transcendent deity, one must struggle to reinterpret the meaning of "truth."

Some of the participationists find such an understanding of truth in the Johannine writings in the New Testament. These writings are the primary locus of the word "truth" (*aletheia*) in the Christian Scriptures, and the uses there are certainly "odd" in comparison with our usual uses, for here there is talk of *doing* the truth and of Jesus' *being* the truth.

Paul S. Minear, in an essay pointing to the role of theopoetic in the Epistle to the Hebrews, notes that the author of that letter misuses, historically speaking, several texts from the Hebrew Scriptures (the Old Testament).

> We have all been trained in the modern academy to spot those errors. Few of us would turn to Hebrews for exact reconstructions of the initial "meanings" of Psalms 8, 22 and Isaiah 8. Often, however, our obsession with those errors has blinded us to the intrinsic authenticity of the hymn, the vision, the poem, which lie beneath and behind the theology of the biblical author. (Minear 1978, 213)

If one accepts the judgment that for Christians "it is the vision, not the doctrine, that communicates to them their identity as God's children and Jesus's brothers" (ibid., 205), what is the task of theology? There is, of course, much room for discussion and disagreement on this question. Nevertheless, it is evident that theology understood as a secondary language of the community of faith is a humbler practice than has often been supposed. Its task is to guide the community in reflection upon the symbols, metaphors, myths, stories, and so on, that have borne the witness which has evoked the faith of the community and its theologians. It does not presume to preside over the dramatic-symbolic means of expression and displace them with supposedly clear definitions of their allegedly vague references to the truth. Rather it responds to and serves those theopoetic expressions, accepting the judgment that doctrinal formulations are never adequate to the truth to which they would help to point. This service includes critical, expository, and constructive functions.

The critical functions of theology so understood include discerning and pointing out (1) when and where the primary language forms of faith (symbol, metaphor, story, myth, etc.) are being misconstrued literalistically or rationalistically; (2) when and where particular forms of those primary modes of faith's expression have lost their power to evoke the experience of grace's judgment and the risking of new or renewed faith; (3) when and where such failures of communication are due to such fundamental cultural changes as to require the abandonment of the old and the discovery of new metaphors, symbols, and so on, as distinguished from the situations in which the community's deafness to those symbolic forms can be "healed"; and (4) when and where new and powerful metaphors, symbols, stories are coming to birth.

The expository functions, which overlap with the critical, are constituted by the teaching and preaching that aid the members of the community to respond to the primary language forms and to reflect constructively and coherently upon them and the experience they mediate, so that we may discern and pursue the kinds of life and conduct that the grace of God would enable.

The constructive function, building upon the critical and expository functions, consists of the continuing effort to reformulate the doctrines, the community's reflective understandings and affirmations of the reality, the activity, and the will of God. It is not done, however, with the supposition that any such reformulation will be the correct statement of the truth of God for us, but in the much more modest search for a relatively more helpful expression of that elusive ubiquitous truth for some people in a particular time and place. This is required by the judgments (1) that the language of academic theology is a secondary language of the church; (2) that language and symbols are historically and culturally relative; (3) that God remains free, gracious, and transcendent; and (4) that we humans are always seeking idolatrous security through trusting something less mysterious than God that we can delude ourselves into thinking is God's truth or will.

The potential importance of such a participationist approach to theology can be illustrated by the interpretations of the person and work of Jesus Christ discussed in relation to their historical and cultural relativity in chapter 1. When, several years ago, a young child asked her Sunday-school teacher whether Jesus was God or the Son of God, she was, quite understandably, treating the religious language as if it were conventional discourse. The teacher could have replied in good orthodox fashion by saying that Jesus was and is God the Son, but such an answer would not be likely to help the child recognize that God-talk does not function like our usual talk of finite creaturely subjects. When one of the participants in the early church disputes about the relation of God the Son to God the Father argued that the two must be co-eternal because otherwise, "before" the Son, God would not have been Father, he was showing the same misunderstanding as does the child's question. Indeed, a great deal of the bitter struggling in the history of Christian doctrines has been a result of this very misunderstanding and its implicit assumption that God is a subject about which we can talk in the same ways as we do when we discuss other matters.

One of the critical tasks of theologians is to discern such misunderstandings. In most cases theologians of rationalistic orientation share this general judgment and hold that our talk of God as Father and Son, for example, is analogical. For those of participationist orientation the misunderstanding is seen as more serious. The critical task involves more than detecting misperceptions of the "logic" of theological and religious language. Part of the critical task includes discerning where the language has ceased to function with dramatic/symbolic power, that is, where it no longer confronts hearers with the challenge to participate in the meaning, to take the risk of faith, to become new persons. To explain the "meanings" of Father and Son as parts of our God-talk by offering "clearer" statements to conscious reason, removing parabolic shock, symbolic power, and narrative invitation, is, from the participationist standpoint, to depart entirely from religious meaning. The statement "Jesus is God" is a very dangerous assertion in our cultural setting, for it does not shock us with its paradoxicality but encourages the false security of the supposition that we have definite metaphysical knowledge of the absolute authority. It comforts some directly with thoughts of Jesus' supposed omniscience and miraculous powers and indirectly with the lawgiving authority and personal irrelevance of that divine being in human appearance.

In the participationist view, such misinterpretations of traditional Christian rhetoric must be unmasked, and ways must be sought to restore dramatic/symbolic/parabolic/mythic/narrative meaning to our efforts to bear witness to the experience of having been confronted by the gracious presence of God in and through the faith community's depictions of Jesus as Christ, Lord, Savior, Shepherd, Son, Brother, Redeemer, Reconciler, Deliverer, Healer, and a host of other story-evoking "names."

It is evidently a characteristic of our culture that it is terribly difficult to see and accept the various and competing traditional interpretations of the "saving work" of Jesus Christ as dramatic narratives that in various times and places have had the symbolic power to evoke trust in the loving presence of God. Instead we seem to need to determine which "theory" is right or to declare all of them wrong. Yet the classical depictions of Jesus Christ as "victor," as "ransom," as "substitute," as "sacrifice," as "satisfaction," and so on, were each powerful vehicles for evoking faith within the cultural settings in which they became prominent, *even though* they cannot be harmonized with each other when they are understood rationalistically and, for many today, communicate an impression contrary to that of a gracious God. Participationist theologians see in these doctrines not logical explanations of Jesus Christ's saving work, but stories, metaphors, symbols that expressed effectively in their own settings the experience of Christians who knew their lives to have been changed radically. It is not the erroneousness of ancient and medieval theologies, but the literalistic and rationalistic misunderstandings of our own time that cut us off from Christian witnesses to whom we are deeply indebted.

If this is true, part of the theologians' task is to show us such misunderstandings, explain the kind of language and meaning intended in each expression of faith, and search for the stories, the metaphors, and the symbols that can open us to such participated meanings. The last is neither a simple nor a secular task. "Any fresh renewal of language or rebirth of images arises from within and from beyond our control. Nevertheless we can help to prepare the event, both by moral and spiritual disciplines and by attention to the modes and vehicles of the Word" (Wilder 1976, 6).

The foregoing discussion of the differences between rationalistic and participationist understandings of the language, meaning, and truth of Christian faith and theology has been one-sided. This is not because the author agrees with the participationist orientation, though he does, but because of the author's judgment that rationalistic assumptions have so dominated the theological life of the church and are so widespread in our culture as not to need the exposition that is, for the very same reasons, required for the participationist viewpoint.

These two orientations are to be found in many and various forms and degrees. They represent, nevertheless, a very important difference of basic perspective. Any thoughtful person who would understand modern theologies in their differences from each other and from popular views of Christian faith must be aware of them.

Recognition of this difference is, however, but one aspect of the need to overcome naiveté about language, meaning, and truth in religion and theology if one is not to be lost in confusion and idolatry. Both the rationalist and the participationist theologians today recognize that language, the essential medium of theological reflection and formulation, is finite, historically and culturally relative, and fraught with ambiguity. Nowhere is this more true than in the field of theology where the subject is the transcendent and mysterious source of all meaning, and where the practitioners are anxiously self-reflective creatures (human beings) both longing for and fearing the presence of God.

WORKS CITED

Betz, H. D.
    1979   *Galatians: A Commentary on Paul's Letter to the Churches in Galatia.* Hermeneia. Philadelphia: Fortress Press.

Braithwaite, R. B.
    1955   *An Empiricist's View of the Nature of Religious Belief.* Cambridge: Cambridge University Press.

Crossan, J. D.
    1973   *In Parables: The Challenge of the Historical Jesus.* New York: Harper & Row.

Funk, R. W.
1966   *Language, Hermeneutic, and Word of God: The Problem of Language in the New Testament and Contemporary Theology.* New York: Harper & Row.

Goldberg, M.
1981   *Theology and Narrative: A Critical Introduction.* Nashville: Abingdon Press.

Minear, P. S.
1978   "An Early Christian Theopoetic?" *Semeia 12*, Part I, edited by W. A. Beardslee, 201–14. Society of Biblical Literature. Missoula, Mont.: Scholars Press.

Petersen, N. R.
1985   *Rediscovering Paul: Philemon and the Sociology of Paul's Narrative World.* Philadelphia: Fortress Press.

Ramsey, I. T.
1957   *Religious Language: An Empirical Placing of Theological Phrases.* London: SCM Press.

Tracy, D., and J. B. Cobb, Jr.
1983   *Talking About God: Doing Theology in the Context of Modern Pluralism.* New York: Seabury Press.

Tugendhat, E.
1967   *Der Wahrheitsbegriff bei Husserl und Heidegger.* Berlin: Walter de Gruyter.

Via, D. O., Jr.
1967   *The Parables: Their Literary and Existential Dimension.* Philadelphia: Fortress Press.

Wilder, A. N.
1971   *Early Christian Rhetoric: The Language of the Gospel.* Cambridge: Harvard University Press.

1976   *Theopoetic: Theology and the Religious Imagination.* Philadelphia: Fortress Press.

5

REAFFIRMING SOVEREIGN GRACE

THERE IS MUCH resistance to modern theology. This is hardly surprising. On the one hand, our religious convictions—unless simply hypocritical—are the foundation and guide of our lives. When they are contested, we are likely to feel threatened and become defensive. On the other hand, the distinguishing characteristics of modern theology constitute an attack upon the kinds of security many have sought in the traditional orthodoxies. Inevitably, many have seen modern theologies as a denial of Christian faith. How can modern theology with all of its disturbing differences from premodern theology serve the same gospel as did the premodern theologies?

THE GOSPEL IN SOME MODERN THEOLOGIES

In order to illustrate the claim that modern theologians are seeking to serve the gospel precisely in the characteristics that distinguish their work from the premodern understandings of the gospel, some prominent examples of current and nontraditional theological proposals will be discussed. The choice of examples is arbitrary, for there are many different approaches and emphases being offered today. Modern theology, unlike some stages of premodern theology, acknowledges no one way of expressing the "message" of Christian faith as the correct one. That message is about God, God-for-us, and it cannot, therefore, be *identified* with any human linguistic formulation, though it may be conveyed for some by various expressions. Modern theology is decidedly pluralistic. This is not simply to say that there are many competing theologies being proposed today, but also to affirm this multiplicity and "competition" as good for the church. Certainly each theologian believes that the theology he or she proposes is the best interpretation possible in the context in which it is proposed, but modern theologians respect one another as participants in the same effort to serve the community of faith and its mission to the world. They recognize that the "good news" concerning God-for-us transcends any and every particular interpretation, and they see, therefore, that they need each other's critical responses.

The purpose of the following examples is not to suggest that these are fully representative of the current theological scene, nor that these are the best proposals being made. It is to illustrate, by way of some current and controversial theological viewpoints, the claim that modern theologians are seeking to aid the church in understanding and obeying and proclaiming the very gospel that was interpreted and proclaimed by the premodern theologians. The examples chosen are (1) process theologies, (2) liberation theologies, and (3) theologies affirming religious pluralism.

Process Theologies

Some basic characteristics of a process theological perspective have been discussed in chapter 2. As noted there, the emphasis on the word "process" indicates that these philosophers and theologians have adopted a new conceptuality (a set of basic concepts) for understanding the nature of reality and therefore of God. Whereas the metaphysics in terms of which classical theologies interpreted the nature and activity of God construed reality as consisting of enduring substances that acted upon each other externally, process thinkers understand reality as organically interrelated events. As modern science has found in the phenomena of human experience, there are no fixed entities. Even a stone, a grain of sand, or an atom is a dynamic process. Its being is temporal and profoundly related to other such dynamic processes. The ancient metaphysics were consistent with human observations of their own times, but they are not consistent with modern scientific understandings. Reality is not a collection of discrete entities, but is an organic process.

The classical theologies that built upon the ancient metaphysical categories described a God outside of time and space. It was a God understood to intervene in world events from beyond all that which constitutes humanly understandable experience. The perfection of God was understood to mean that God could not be affected by anything outside "himself," for that would introduce contingency (imperfection) into God. Therefore God was believed already to know all, including what for us is the future. Such an understanding undermines belief in human freedom and responsibility, and it suggests an implacable Deity which might well be feared, but which it is useless to pray to and inappropriate to worship.

Process theologies have proclaimed God as a part of the process that reality is, eminent within it and different from the creatures, but subject to the structures of reality including temporality. God is described as being both absolute and relative, absolute in the divine primordial nature (thus not subject to death or to fundamental change of nature), and relative in the divine consequent nature, experiencing ("prehending") all the events of reality. God is thus affected by the events of our lives, knows of them and cares about them.

Opponents of process thought see this reinterpretation of the nature of God as denying divine transcendence and perfection and thereby reducing the concept of God such that faith is not possible. How can persons risk utter trust in another contingent and temporal being? Such a finite God, limited by the structures of reality and always limited in creativity by the present state of the creation, may know and care about and remember us, but the sovereign power in which utter trust can be placed is lacking. This judgment finds support in the denial of eternal life explicit in some process theologians' writings (Hamilton 1967, 122–33; Hartshorne 1967, 55–56, 112). The inference is that the finite God of process thought, being subject to the basic structures of reality, *cannot* overcome the death of the creatures. Whereas more traditional Christian theologies understand God to transcend the basic structures of the creation as their source, and therefore to have options beyond this cosmos, the creativity of process thought's God is limited by those structures. God's being, though eminent in the whole of finite reality, is nevertheless *within* it. Thus some process theologians affirm what they call "objective immortality." Contrary to what that sounds like, it does not mean that any person will live beyond death, but that God will *remember* all persons, because all events are prehended in God's consequent nature.

On this last point it must be noted that not all process theologians agree with the denial of "eternal life." Some of them judge that this is a question which must be left open (Cobb and Griffin 1976, 123–24; Ogden 1963, 226–29). As Ogden expresses it, the God of Christian faith is pure unbounded love, so we can set no limits to God's mercies. We can know that we will be a part of God's everlasting life (for God has prehended our lives), but we are not in a position to know whether the divine love will grant experiencing subjects some kind of survival of death.

Thus, while process theologians affirm a God who is limited, it is not necessary to conclude that such limits render God impotent in relation to any essential human need. Those who follow closely Charles Hartshorne's claim to be able to prove the reality of God have thereby a more specifically limited deity, and it may be that for this definition of God the power to overcome death for individual persons is lacking. But this is not clearly the case for A. N. Whitehead's depiction of God. Whitehead does not claim to prove God, and his philosophical perspective is much less bound to logic and more open to symbolic meaning than is Hartshorne's. Even if this were not true, Christian theologians who make use of the thought categories developed by such philosophers are not bound to follow those philosophers strictly, for as Christian theologians they speak out of their participation in the community of faith. They seek to interpret that faith by the aid of the conceptuality, but faith's commitment is prior.

Thus, the process theologians employ the process concepts not only because they judge that those concepts are more true to modern understanding of reality and human experience, but even more because they believe that God as described in process categories is more in keeping with the experience of faith. Christian faith does not relate to a static God who, because perfect, is beyond being affected by our lives, but to a caring and compassionate God who takes our lives up into the divine life.

On these last points there is much agreement. Although there are yet some Christian theologians who affirm "divine impassibility" (that God cannot be affected from outside), neither they nor the majority who deny that doctrine intend to affirm a static, implacable, uncaring deity. All are agreed that God is a living and caring presence and that God and only God is worthy of worship. The difference is on the question of how this may be most coherently understood and expressed. The defenders of the classical Christian conceptuality point out that the understanding of being and of God therein is not static but, in fact, dynamic. Process thinkers point out that however much academic truth there may be in that interpretation, the classical categories do not today convey the meaning of God as living, caring, and compassionate. They see serious inconsistency between that conceptuality and the daily prayer life of believers.

In addition to those who argue the relative merits of these two metaphysical systems as conceptual vehicles for understanding Christian faith (and those who offer other metaphysical views), there are many in theology today who argue that Christian theology should espouse no particular metaphysical system. Usually the basic view of these theologians is that God transcends the structures of any and every human attempt to describe the nature of reality, so that we can never describe the being or life of God in itself but can at best seek to depict faith's experience of God by analogy, symbol, metaphor, and so on. Here again, there is a longstanding and continuing debate, the defenders of particular metaphysical theories arguing that without such a theory vagueness, inconsistency, and incoherence are inevitable, and their opponents arguing that such metaphysical commitments presume to place human limits upon God. In the view of some of these last, there is usefulness in each of the metaphysical interpretations proposed as long as it is not supposed that any one of them is *the* right interpretation, for God is greater than any or all of them can describe.

There is not going to be a solution to these disagreements here—or anywhere else. The point to be noted is that deeper than these disagreements is agreement. In this context there is agreement that God is experienced in Christian faith as a living, caring, compassionate, and responding presence who alone is worthy of utter human trust. Even these words, however, cannot escape the problems that have been described above. They are historically, culturally, and even individually relative. They cannot escape ambiguity. They, too, have been "domesticated," so the meaning they intend may now be impeded by them. This is one of the reasons why the debates among these theologians are an important service to the community of faith, and why the freedom to continue those debates is essential for the health of that community.

Liberation Theologies

Liberation theologies are to be found in a much greater variety than are process theologies. There are black liberation theologies, women's liberation theologies, Native American liberation theologies, and varieties of Third World liberation theologies. Within each of these groupings there are significantly differing theological proposals.

In all of this variety, however, there are basic common characteristics that justify the single broad label. They all seek to reinterpret Christian faith from the standpoint of oppressed persons, seeking to show that God revealed in Jesus Christ an utter opposition to oppression of human beings and called persons to join in the cause of liberation. They point out that though Jesus and the apostles were identified with the disadvantaged and the downtrodden and the early church was subject to oppression, for most of its subsequent history Christianity has been aligned with privilege and power. For the most part, it is persons who have been participants in this world of status and acceptance who have been the churches' theological interpreters. Education has been by and for the privileged in the developed nations. Inevitably the "correct" understandings of Christian faith have been declared by the representatives of the establishment to the second-class citizens of the world. Theology has been an activity (with but few exceptions until recently) of male white citizens of Europe and North America. It is hardly surprising, therefore, that in large measure the work of the theologians has supported—overtly or subtly—the established economic, social, and political structures, and has done little to evoke widespread concern about the dehumanization of women, of nonwhites, and of the poor, whether in developed or underdeveloped nations.

There have been notable exceptions to such generalizations, and the call for self-giving love of one's neighbors, especially the downtrodden, is to be found in the theologies, the liturgies, the hymns, and the preaching of most Christian groups. These exceptions, however, indicate but another reason for the search for a liberationist reinterpretation of Christian faith, for there is a contradiction here. Christian congregations sing of concern for the oppressed

in the name of Jesus Christ who identified himself with the poor and the outcast and was executed by the privileged and the powerful, but the members
of those congregations are not often moved to any such sacrifice on behalf of
suffering neighbors. The Christian congregations are usually a comfortable
part of the social, political, and economic structures which maintain—even if
unwittingly—the hopelessness of the poor, the weak, and the exploited, *and
those congregations are unaware of any contradiction in this.* In effect, the traditional theological and liturgical formulations are not confronting us with the
judgment and the gift of the gospel, even though such words as "judgment"
and "calls to suffering and sacrifice on behalf of neighbor" are present.
Again, the language has been domesticated. It does not matter that academically this language can be defended, for, as a matter of fact, it is not communicating the gospel.

There is nothing surprising, therefore, in the fact that there has been—
and continues to be—great opposition to liberation theologies. They are by
the nature of their aims "revolutionary," in the sense that they seek basic
change in social, economic, and political structures in order to bring about
the liberation of the oppressed. This necessarily entails threats to the comfort
and security of the more fortunate, and it pronounces judgment upon us in
the name of our Lord! In general, there is no way in which we can deny the
validity of this and its value for us, but much basis is found for denial of the
particular ways in which it is done. Some liberation theologians refuse to condemn violence in the cause of liberation, and we recall Jesus' condemnations
of violence. Some liberation theologians appeal to the teachings of Karl
Marx, and we infer that they must be atheistic materialists and communists.
Some liberation theologians speak of God as "Mother" and use the pronoun
"she" in reference to the Deity, and we insist upon the biblical and traditional affirmations that God is our "Father." How can such teachings be defended as efforts to reformulate our doctrines in order to make clearer the
judgment and the promise of the gospel? Are they not rather ideologies using
Christian talk as support for the political, economic, and social aspirations of
particular groups of persons?

This last charge, that liberation theologies are really ideologies rather than
genuine theologies, is a common one that has been applied to all types of liberation theology. The term "ideology" as used here refers to the basic doctrines of a particular group or movement or institution. The distinction of an
ideology from a genuine theology can be expressed most easily in two complementary ways. (1) An ideology does not seek to serve the will of God but
to use talk of the will of God to serve the desires of persons. The question
here is a very basic one of priority. (2) An ideology, in distinction from a
sound Christian theology, seeks the well-being of some particular group of
persons rather than of all. It is easy to see how a liberation theology could be

no more than an ideology. There is a focus upon the need to overcome the systems and circumstances that are dehumanizing certain groups of persons. Those who are seen to be directly or indirectly responsible for the dehumanizing are readily identified as "the enemy," whose existence as children of God (also) who are being dehumanized by their own complicity in dehumanizing others is easily forgotten in the struggle for change and/or in the rhetoric calling for change. If the proponents of betterment for the poor call for the destruction of the rich, or if the would-be deliverers of nonwhite peoples from destructive racist structures are willing for the destruction of white people, or if feminists seek the subjugation of males as the means to freedom from sexist repression, are these not ideological programs rather than Christian theological interpretations of the will of God manifest in Jesus Christ? Surely the answer is yes.

That, however, is no refutation of liberation theologies. Although examples can be found in which proponents of each of these changes have used Christian theological language to support calls to reverse the roles of the oppressors and the oppressed, or have at least used rhetoric to this effect, there is nothing about the desire for elimination of oppression and dehumanization that requires such limited and contradictory aims, and they would clearly be incompatible with Christian faith.

The writings of the prominent black liberation theologian James Cone (b. 1938) offer a helpful illustration of these issues. If one pays attention only to certain more strident statements (more strident, that is, to "white" ears), it is easy to make a prima facie case that his teaching is more ideological than truly theological. One of his books is entitled *God of the Oppressed,* and that title is the book's central theological affirmation, that God *is* the God of the oppressed. Jesus Christ is the Liberator of the oppressed. The apparent implication that God is the God *only* of the oppressed and Jesus Christ the Liberator *only* of the oppressed is enforced by such statements as ". . . Israel's election cannot be separated from her servitude and liberation. Here God discloses that he is the God of history whose will is identical with the liberation of the oppressed from social and political bondage. The doing of theology, therefore, on the basis of the revelation of Yahweh, must involve the politics which takes its stand with the poor and against the rich" (Cone 1975, 65). "For if the essence of the Gospel *is* the liberation of the oppressed from sociopolitical humiliation for a new freedom in Christ Jesus (and I do not see how anyone can read the Scriptures and conclude otherwise), and if Christian theology is an explication of the meaning of that Gospel for our time, must not theology itself have liberation as its starting point or run the risk of being at best idle talk and at worst blasphemy?" (ibid., 51–52). "The convergence of Jesus Christ and the black experience is the meaning of the Incarnation. Because God became man in Jesus Christ, he disclosed the divine will to be with humanity in our wretchedness. And because we blacks accept his presence in Jesus as the true definition of our humanity, blackness and divinity are dialectically bound together as one reality" (ibid., 35). Christ is said to be black, both literally and symbolically. "To say that Christ is black means that black people are God's poor people whom Christ has come to liberate" (ibid., 136). He has come to liberate them from the bondage imposed by "racism, that demon embedded in white folks' being . . ." (ibid., 156).

It is unfair and misleading, however, to take these statements out of their full context in order to give the impression that this book offers an ideological use of Christian language in support of the worldly hopes and aims of some people rather than as an interpretation of the will and love of God for all persons. In the same book Cone also affirms that "*all* are oppressed (and especially those who rule over others), . . ." and "the oppressed must therefore fight against the oppressors in order to fight for them. . . . To recognize that liberation is for oppressors because it is for all people prevents hate and revenge from destroying the revolutionary struggle" (ibid., 148, 151). Not only are the oppressors not excluded from God's love (except as they exclude themselves in their oppressing), neither is liberation seen in only social, political, and economic terms. Cone insists that the freedom given by Christ's liberation is more than the freedom made possible in history (ibid., 80), but in opposing everything dehumanizing, it *also* calls for freedom *in* history.

As Cone indicates, the central message that God is shown in Jesus Christ to be the God of the oppressed (not implying that God is not also shown to be God of the oppressors but showing them to shut out divine grace) is not new. That message is pervasive in the Bible. That there was not a social ethic in a modern sense in much of Christian history may be seen to be related to the expectation of a supernatural termination to history—always expected "soon," and to the circumstances in which the means of production and distribution were not sufficient to offer the kinds of worldly possibilities that have emerged in the modern era. Nevertheless, there were notable instances in which Christian leaders such as Saint Francis and John Wesley recognized that Jesus' own identification with the disadvantaged was relevant to his disciples, and the social gospel movement is only the most prominent among several modern theological efforts to confront Christians with this truth.

That message has also been alive in the United States. It may be seen as a remarkable achievement of black American preachers and teachers that they were able to communicate to those living under the terrible deprivations of American slavery and then "Jim Crowism" that the Lord proclaimed in Christian faith—the religion (at least verbally) of the oppressors—was *for them,* was and is God of the oppressed. It seems to be a more common view among Americans in general today that only when things are going as we want them to can we suppose that "somebody up there likes me!" The success of black American theology in maintaining the contrary may well be the most impressive accomplishment of American theology up to this time.

As some of the liberationists have pointed out in response to the charges that liberation theologies are really ideologies, traditional Christian theological formulations have themselves clearly been ideological. At least they have been used to maintain oppressive and dehumanizing systems and structures. Slavery, racism, sexism, and the perpetuating of grinding poverty have all been defended in the name of Jesus Christ. This, of course, is more easily seen by the oppressed than by the oppressors, for the natural human motivation of self-protectiveness operates to make it clear to the former and to hide it from the latter. We human beings are adept at rationalizing what we want to believe, and at being blind to what we do not want to see. As Cone pointedly remarks, "Because white theologians are well fed and speak for a people who control the means of production, the problem of hunger is not a theological issue for them. That is why they spend more time debating the relation between the Jesus of history and the Christ of faith than probing the depths of Jesus' command to feed the poor" (ibid., 52). Usually we hasten to point defensively to exceptions to this claim and explain the importance of the academic issue, for we are not eager to hear the judgment of the gospel. Any theology that is able to communicate meaningfully the divine love for the world's unloved will be heard first as judgment by those implicated in the oppressions.

Consider the enormous resistance to the use of feminine terms in reference to God. What can the reason be? Often it has been pointed out that not only tradition but the Scriptures speak of God almost exclusively in masculine terms, and according to the New Testament, Jesus, himself a male and known to Christian faith as "God the Son Incarnate," not only spoke of God as Father, but used the intimate term *Abba*, sometimes translated as "Daddy." This seems to be one of the very distinctive aspects of Jesus' teaching. As long as it could be assumed that the Scriptures were direct and divinely controlled communication from God and that whatever those writings reported as having been said by Jesus was God's speaking, this argument was very convincing. That there were some biblical passages that referred to God in feminine terms was usually unnoticed, and little was made of it. With the recognition of the human and historical character of the Scriptures, however, it became possible to see that in the Bible's predominantly male references to God we have but a manifestation of the inevitable style of interpretation in a thoroughly paternalistic society. It is human witness that takes this form, not the revelation itself.

It takes little reflection to note that God cannot be supposed to be a male. Masculinity and femininity are designations of a finite creaturely distinction, and it is a distinction of two incomplete representations of a species in which each is in need of the other if the species is to survive. The term is strictly inappropriate for designating that in which faith trusts. As long as it was possible to maintain the belief that women were inferior to men, that only the latter and not the former were fully human, it was easy to suppose that male references for God were the best available for indicating the personal character of faith's experience of God. Yet now that this belief in male superiority has been shown untenable, the same supposition continues.

It is difficult to see any better reasons for this than habit and prejudice. Those are, of course, strong motivations in spite of their being unreasonable. If the habit and prejudice are indications of idolatrous comfort, the motivation is both very powerful and very serious. It is then a part of the general responsibility of the church's theologians to reveal and seek to overcome the idolatry. When it is further seen that the maintaining of the male God image offers an incomplete symbol for God, undercutting the possibilities of faith for both males and females, and also undergirds the continued disadvantaging and dehumanizing of women, the need to overcome the idolatry may be recognized as critical.

Just how this overcoming may be accomplished is not self-evident. If one has a very rationalistic understanding of religious and theological meanings, it might be fairly easy simply to explain the errors of male sexist prejudice in religion and society, and, noting the inadequacy of both male and female designations for God, either avoid them or use both as evenhandedly as possible. Some kinds of prejudice seem to surrender to education, but there is ample evidence that many do not. If religious and theological meanings are more of the "participationist" character, so that references to God as Father or as Mother have either symbolic power or fail to communicate as intended, there will be no simple solution. Theologians will struggle to discern where symbols are dying and where they are emerging. They will seek depth metaphors that can break through the idolatrously functioning "domesticated" language, and they will find out by observation—not by theory—what are the more helpful ways of portraying and proclaiming the holy, mysterious, and gracious Spirit.

It is therefore understandable that there are varieties of "feminist liberation theologies" today. The processes in which they are in dialogue and debate with each other and with other theological emphases are both creative and protective for the community of faith, the community whose life will gradually show which are the more fruitful proposals. Once again, it should be possible to recognize, even in so brief a sketch of complex and varied proposals and arguments, that feminist theologies today are not only compatible with the gospel but demanded by it.

Liberation theologies are many and various. They are as subject to error and excess as are all other theologies. To reject them altogether on the basis of the common charges is readily seen as an expression of the self-protective anxiety that accompanies idolatry. The basic characteristic of liberation theologies—their commitment to seek an end to dehumanizing systems and structures—is the real source of the general opposition, for the privileged fear that they will suffer if the present systems and structures are changed. A judgment about how helpful to the church of Jesus Christ in its mission to the world any particular liberation theology is can only be responsibly attempted through the same processes by which any specific theological proposal should be evaluated. It should not be difficult to see, however, that any theology that is not centrally concerned with communicating God's love for all peoples and God's judgment upon oppression and dehumanization would be most difficult to defend as a Christian theology. It is hard to avoid the judgment that the basic impulse of liberation theologies is consistent with the Christian gospel.

Christian Theological Affirmations of Religious Pluralism

"Religious pluralism" is not a reference to the pluralism in Christian theology today which, as noted above, is applauded by modern theologians as a benefit to the church. To speak of a Christian theological affirmation of "religious pluralism" is to indicate that an increasing number of modern theologians are judging that the God whom we know through the church's witness to Jesus Christ has also been known in and through other world religions. It is therefore also to repudiate the exclusivism that has characterized Christian history.

By "Christian exclusivism" is meant the belief that only Christians are or will be included within "the kingdom of God," that "outside the church (or of Christianity) there is no salvation," so any persons who fail to become Christians are "lost" or "condemned." Until very recently the common exclusivisms were often more narrow yet. It was common for Protestants and Roman Catholics each to judge the other "heretics," and "disciples of the anti-Christ," and there are still places where this is true. There are yet some denominations that affirm that they only are the true church. So it is hardly surprising that there is much resistance to the idea that Christians might affirm persons of other religions as possibly reconciled to God, and participants in God's realm. That resistance is not, however, simply a matter of habit and prejudice.

Christian exclusivism has been an inherent aspect of traditional Christian theologies. In the medieval church the very possibility of receiving saving grace was dependent upon participation in the sacraments—except for "the extraordinary means of grace" of which humans have no knowledge. More centrally, the theories of atonement—whether by ransom from, defeat of, or deception of the devil, or by substitutionary sacrifice and satisfaction of the divine honor—understood the salvation of humankind to be dependent upon God's supernatural intervention in Jesus Christ and human knowledge of that saving event to be dependent upon God's supernatural inspiration of Scripture and creed and guidance of the church. Any "Old Testament" figures understood to have been accepted by God were believed either to have been saved through Jesus Christ or under terms of a "dispensation" that was ended by the Christ-event.

The interpretation of Christian faith in terms of supernatural causal intervention which was assumed in premodern theologies does not strictly require exclusivism, and during much of the history of Christianity no such general repudiation of other "faiths" (the concept of "religions" is a relatively recent Western concept) was officially declared. Different attitudes were taken toward each "faith" at various times. Nevertheless, the conviction that God had acted in Jesus Christ in a decisive, essential, and final way made christocentric exclusivism a natural and almost inevitable inference. It is therefore hardly surprising that traditional Christian theologies have been exclusivistic or that many Christians today are disturbed by the rejections of such exclusivism in some modern theologies. The attachment to the traditional interpretations becomes even more powerful where it is idolatrous, for there is a marked tendency for anxious believers to find a source of supposed security in the belief that "my way is the only way; I am saved and they are damned."

Christian exclusivism, however, is by no means to be judged as a merely popular misrepresentation of Christian faith. Karl Barth, possibly the most influential Protestant theologian of this century, set forth a basis for exclusivism that dominated much of the theological discussion for many years. He argued that Christianity is not a religion. "Religion" is (in his view) a term referring to human attempts to relate to God, attempts which, therefore, must be recognized to be sinful. Christian faith is the result of God's grace and initiative. Insofar as those who call themselves Christians are practicing religion, that is, trying to make their peace with God by their own efforts, they are not persons of Christian faith. In Christ, God has offered the gift of faith. If we are faithful, we know that that is not our doing, and we can only be grateful. It is to be affirmed that God's grace is toward all and sovereign over all, but that is no grounds for affirming human religions, according to Barth.

Under the influence of this Barthian perspective, a large percentage of Christian theologians were not even concerned to study non-Christian "faiths" during much of this century. This, however, has changed dramatically in recent years. When the historical and cultural relativity of all theological formulations, including those of Scripture and tradition, is recognized, all issues are subject to reexamination, and when the assumption of supernatural causal intervention becomes questionable, exclusivism is likewise subject to doubt. Although they are probably still a minority, a growing number of modern Christian theologians are concluding either that Christian faith does not require exclusivistic claims or that it is not even compatible with them. For example, in a series of articles by a wide variety of well-known theological writers who responded to a request from *The Christian Century* to discuss how their theological thinking had developed particularly during the decade of the 1970s, half of the twenty Christian theologians included the denial of Christian exclusivism and the affirmation of other religions in their responses (Wall 1981). Just how such a departure from traditional Christian convictions may be seen as consistent with the Christian gospel can be illustrated by a brief look at treatments of this question by various modern theologians.

The influential German Roman Catholic theologian Karl Rahner (1904–84) argued against Christian exclusivism (with its simple repudiation of other religions) precisely on the grounds that the grace of God manifest in Jesus Christ requires the recognition that God's grace is at work in other religions. Nature and grace do not simply stand outside each other. God, the Creator of nature, is by divine free choice present to and in nature in self-giving. Therefore a non-Christian religion is not limited to distorted natural knowledge of God. "It contains also supernatural elements arising out of the grace which is given to men as a gratuitous gift on account of Christ" (Rahner 1966, 121). The Christian's knowledge of God's gracious will for the salvation of all humankind means that the possibility of a saving relationship to God must be and have been present in all human times and situations (ibid., 128). Rahner proposed (without suggesting that all religious faiths are equal and there is no need for Christian missions) that Christians should recognize that persons of other religious faiths may be seen as "anonymous Christians" (ibid., 131).

So, "the Church will not so much regard herself today as the exclusive community of those who have a claim to salvation but rather as the historically tangible vanguard and the historically and socially constituted explicit expression of what the Christian hopes is present as a hidden reality even outside the visible Church" (ibid., 133). Rahner was emphatic in his insistence that Christianity is the one absolute religion intended by God for all persons (ibid., 118). Other religions, though they exist in response to the grace of God and have validity in relation to salvation, are by no means equal to Christianity. It is the Incarnation of God's gracious self-giving in Jesus Christ that constitutes this distinctiveness and superiority in relation to other religions, but it is also this self-manifestation of God in Jesus Christ that enables Christians to recognize that the grace of God is both sovereign and ubiquitous and always at work in human lives. Therefore, "the Church is not the communion of those who possess God's grace as opposed to those who lack it, but it is the communion of those who can explicitly confess what they and the others hope to be. . . . The Church will go out to meet the non-Christian of tomorrow with the attitude expressed by St. Paul when he said: What therefore you do not know and yet worship (and yet *worship!*) that I proclaim to you (Ac 17.23). On such a basis one can be tolerant, humble and yet firm towards all non-Christian religions" (ibid., 134).

Paul Tillich also taught that for Christians it is made manifest in Jesus Christ that the whole of created reality is pervaded by the graciously self-given presence of God, and that every religion is based on actual revelation. He did not, however, agree with the judgment that Christianity is the absolute religion intended by God for all persons. This would hardly be possible in a theology that eschewed the idea of God's acting by supernatural causal intervention. But Tillich did not espouse an utter relativism regarding religions either. In his *Systematic Theology*, he argued that Christian theology is *the* theology because of its doctrine that the Logos became flesh. The "Logos" is the self-revealing reality of God, so, in Tillich's view, every religion is—at root—a response to the Logos. The distinction of Christianity is the affirmation that the Logos was embodied (incarnate) in a person, Jesus, who is therefore the Christ. The Logos is of universal significance. It is the reality of God for everyone in all times. Doctrines of this transcendent reality give it some particularity, so that it becomes understandable for us. Events in which persons or communities are encountered by the Logos give greater specificity, but that gain in meaningfulness is accompanied by a loss in universality. The particularities that make it more significant for one historical-cultural setting make it less meaningful to others. The claim, however, that the Logos became incarnate, was embodied in a particular human life, means that here the Logos is manifest as absolutely universal and absolutely concrete at the same time. Nothing is more concrete for human beings than a human being. In a human life every dimension of being that can be meaningful to us is present. A manifestation in an angel, for example, would not reveal God to us more fully, but less, for whatever an angelic life might be, it is not open to our participation. Yet, though a human life is most concrete for us, in embodying the Logos (the self-revealing reality of God) it is also universal—meaningful for all persons and communities. It is the form of revelation that cannot be transcended. It is qualitatively final. Christianity, then, as the religion based upon this claim, understands itself to be the community of witness to God's "final" (nontranscendable) revelation (Tillich 1951, 16–17).

In Tillich's judgment, this does not make Christianity the absolute religion. That would be idolatry. Christianity, as a religion or a community of faith, is itself historically and culturally conditioned, and as a community of persons, it is subject to distortions. But Christianity points to that which is absolute: the Logos of God.

Non-Christian religions are thus affirmed as rooted in the revelation of God, but they are not judged to be equal. None so much as claims to be a response to such a "concrete universal," to the incarnation of the Logos. When Christians seek understanding of and community with persons of other religions, as the grace of God enables and calls them to do, they listen with love, but not without a basis for distinguishing the truth from the human distortions in the other religions. The biblical depiction of Jesus as the Christ is the *norm* by which Christians assess all truth claims, whether such claims be doctrinal or moral or embodied (lived) "claims" of human wholeness.

The Tillichian position (in which he denied the absoluteness of Christianity claimed by theologians such as Rahner but affirmed a finality to Christianity's distinctive basis and witness) was altered by him in the final lecture of his life in 1965. He had by this time visited Japan where he had been in dialogue with Buddhist scholars, and he had participated for two years with Mircea Eliade in seminars in the history of religions at the University of Chicago. In this final lecture, delivered at that university, he indicated that were he now to rewrite his *Systematic Theology* under the impact of this engagement with world religions, there would be significant differences (Tillich 1966, 91). He emphasized here that revelation is *always* received in distorted form, and went on to say that "there may be—and I stress this, there *may* be—a central event in the history of religions which unites the positive results of those critical developments in the history of religion in and under which revelatory experiences are going on—an event which therefore makes possible a concrete theology that has universalistic significance" (ibid., 81). The confident claim to "finality" had become tentative.

This did not change Tillich's insistence that Christians enter dialogue with other religious traditions with a norm derived from the New Testament's witness to Jesus as the Christ (ibid., 89), for it is the event of Jesus as the Christ through which we have been reconciled to God. Tillich had, however, become much more conscious of the degree to which all Christian witnessing to that event has been historically and culturally conditioned. If we do not struggle to keep *our understandings* of God's self-revelation subject to the criterion of the cross of Jesus Christ, we will bring a cultural prejudice to the conversations that will make it impossible for us to hear the Word of God speaking in and through these other communities founded upon it. In this case, we will not just judge false what is contrary to Christ, but whatever is alien to our cultural conditioning. The "finality" for us of the revelation in Jesus Christ does not require the judgment beforehand that there is less openness to God in the lives of all persons of other religions. It requires of us an openness to such neighbors that may enable us to learn from them—even of the grace of God, for the encounter with deeply differing cultural conditionings may enable us to see yet more of the reality of God embodied in Jesus Christ. It is Jesus Christ, not our interpretations of Jesus Christ, who remains *for us* the criterion. It is the grace of God made known to us in Jesus

Christ that enables us to love and listen to persons of other religions, even to discern in them the "fruits of the Spirit."

John B. Cobb, Jr. (b. 1925), a prominent American Protestant process theologian, has for several years been developing the importance for Christian theology of serious dialogue with other religious traditions. In his book *Christ in a Pluralistic Age*, he discusses the difficulties and possible benefits of such mutual involvement of Christians and Buddhists.

Like Rahner and Tillich, Cobb insists that the Christian must come to such interreligious encounters with a firm recognition of and commitment to Jesus as the Christ, the embodiment of the eternal Logos of God. Judging, however, that the traditional categories employed by theologians such as Rahner and Tillich, even though reinterpreted, are no longer adequate to our experience, he proposes an understanding of Christ in terms of "creative transformation." "'Christ' is understood as the power of transformation, redemption, unification, and order as that power has been apprehended through Jesus and his historical effects" (Cobb 1975, 43). Those historical effects have, however, largely been lost as Christians have fixed their loyalties upon particular forms of witness, doctrine, and ethical teaching, failing to realize that the divine Logos transcends all such historically and culturally relative expressions. This absolutizing of the relative has shut out the very power of creative transformation that those particular forms were intended to convey. "To name the Logos 'Christ' is to express and to elicit trust. It is to promise that the unknown into which we are called is life rather than death. In short, it is to call for and make possible radical conversion from bondage to the past to openness to the future. This to say that to name the Logos 'Christ' is to recognize that the cosmic Logos is love" (ibid., 85).

If we accept the call to faith in Christ, we will not hide defensively in the doctrines and perspectives that we have inherited, but neither will we pretend that we have some neutral position from which to judge the strengths and weaknesses of the world's religions. "The more deeply we trust Christ, the more openly receptive we will be to wisdom from any source, and the more responsibly critical we will be both of our own received habits of mind and of the limitations and distortions of others" (Cobb 1985, 373). Faith makes possible both standing firmly in one's own traditions and being genuinely open to learning from profoundly different traditions, and the challenge of such encounters provides an opportunity for a new creative transformation (a renewed openness to Christ) of one's tradition, one's life, and one's community.

In the light of such an understanding of Christian faith, Cobb discusses the possibilities present in Christian-Buddhist dialogue. He does not overlook the profound differences between the two understandings of the nature of reality and the means of salvation. In Christianity selfhood is intensified, as we are called to take responsibility for who we are and what we do and to love our neighbors precisely in their otherness. In Buddhism the centrality of the self is removed, as anxiety is overcome in detachment and serenity (Cobb 1975, 208). Nevertheless, Cobb suggests that each can be moved by the other's basic image, and each can recognize therein a lack in itself. Buddhism's way of salvation has entailed a kind of nonattention to the world which encouraged neither science nor social ethics. Christianity's emphasis upon personal selfhood seems to have heightened anxiety and alienation, and, with the fading of the traditional God-images, has left many of its adherents feeling alone and isolated. The Buddhist can see value in Christian responsibility, and the Christian can see value in Buddhist serenity. Together the possibilities for creative transformation of each through open dialogue can be discerned, even if it is not yet possible to see how the two can become one (ibid., 208–9).

Cobb argues that the encounter with Judaism is the one that is the most disturbing for Christians. This seems surprising at first, for we often speak of the Judeo-Christian tradition, acknowledging that Christianity arose out of Judaism. But that is part of the problem that Cobb sees for Christians. We have supposed that we have the wisdom of Judaism within Christianity, even that we have understood it better than they! But this arrogance is undergirded by suppressed guilt for the long history of Christian persecution of Jews. We do not want to acknowledge any responsibility for the fact that "the one who for us is the symbol and bearer of liberation, transformation, and reconciliation is for the Jew the symbol of oppression, abuse, and persecution. The Jew knows the underside of our history, the half that we have repressed" (Cobb 1985, 374). As long as we refuse to admit to ourselves these facts of Christian history (and so much in the Christian present), we will remain victims of our own suppressions and repressions, and we will remain a danger to the Jews.

But no answer is to be found in hiding our allegiance to Christ. For us the healing must come in and through Christ, and only as we are healed in Christ can we become agents of the overcoming of enmity between Christ and the Jews. It is a dialogue of the greatest difficulty and the utmost importance for both parties (ibid., 375). It is the love of God, known and unknown, heard and unheard, affirmed and denied in both traditions, that calls for and makes possible this dialogue.

Wilfred Cantwell Smith (b. 1916), Harvard professor of the Comparative History of Religion, in his book *Towards a World Theology*, approaches the affirmation of religious pluralism from a somewhat different angle and goes yet further in his proposals for theology. Rather than addressing the question on the basis of a doctrine of God's presence throughout creation, Smith grounds his proposal in a knowledge of the history of religions. He does not claim to see there a unity of religions. He notes that in fact there is not even unity in one religion! What he does see is a unity of religious history. The religions are not equal, nor even similar, but they are historically interconnected. "What they [the world's religions] have in common is that the history of each has been what it has been in significant part because the history of the others has been what *it* has been" (Smith 1981, 6). Smith proceeds to illustrate this claim in several ways, the most striking of which concerns a fable from the lives of the Christian saints which played a crucial role in the Christian conversion of Leo Tolstoi. Smith traces this story back to Islamic, Manichean, Buddhist, and Hindu or Jain sources! Even the name of the Christian saint of the story, Josaphat, is shown to be a reference to Gautama when he was a future Buddha (ibid., 6–9). The religions that are divided by their histories are also united by their histories. This is not only true of minor and accidental points, Smith affirms, for ". . . every religious tradition on earth has in fact developed in interaction with the others" (ibid., 15). Even ". . . the Christian idea of God in its course over the centuries has been, the historian can now see, a part of the world history of the idea of God on earth, Christians receiving from, contributing to and participating in that total history" (ibid., 16).

Smith by no means suggests that this discovery by the historians of religions provides an easy route to religious unity. Quite the contrary, he seeks to show how a Muslim, a Buddhist, a Hindu, and a Jew would each have great difficulties with what he is urging in this book, their basic outlooks being profoundly different from the Christian in certain important respects (ibid., 130–51). Smith's proposal is that we should be working toward a "world theology," an understanding of faith that is particular to each tradition's experience, but which also transcends the limits of each. The suggestion is not that we Christians develop a Christian interpretation of Islam, Judaism, and so on. Smith insists that a Christian interpretation of another faith would necessarily be a misinterpretation, just as a Muslim interpretation of Christian faith would be a misinterpretation, for in each such case the categories of interpretation would be alien to that which is interpreted. What must be sought, Smith believes, is a "disciplined corporate self-consciousness, critical, comprehensive, global," a humane knowing that requires participation rather than objectifying, a knowing in which each participant becomes a new kind of person, and through which humankind moves toward becoming one community (ibid., 78–79).

Through a lifetime spent as a Christian seeking to understand persons of other religious traditions, Smith has become convinced that the claim that only Christian faith saves is neither true nor consistent with Christian faith. If one asks, for example, whether God has spoken to Muslims through the Qur'an, Smith's answer is

that on any given morning in Baghdad or Jogjakarta or Timbuktu, in this century or that, the faith of a particular Muslim, member of a particular society, had
a specific form constituted by his participation in the Islamic context of his life
that was that particular moment of the total process of the Islamic strand in world
religious history; and that in that faith in that particular form he was in touch
with God, and God with him. God spoke to him; more or less clearly, more or
less effectively, with more or less response—in a voice muffled by the din of dis-
tracting worldly beguilements and inner personal deflections, muffled also by the
perennial inadequacies of the channels available to Him, muffled by the limited
capacity of man to hear; none the less, He spoke, and He was heard. (Ibid.,
164–65)

Smith hastens to note that he would not idealize the Muslim. He recognizes
in him a sinner like himself, one who, in Luther's formula, is justified and
yet sinful, that is, a human being of faith. Smith does not write here simply as
a scholar studying books, but as a Christian who has struggled to enter into
the lives of persons of other traditions, persons in whom he has found the
"fruits of the Spirit." He therefore argues that though faith differs in form, it
does not differ in kind (ibid., 168), and the discovery that God saves through
these differing forms "corroborates our Christian vision of God as active in
history, redemptive, reaching out to all men to love and to embrace them"
(ibid., 171).

It is not being suggested here that all modern Christian theologians agree
with this call of W. C. Smith to work toward a world theology, nor that a
majority agree with any of the theological positions affirming religious pluralism. It does seem clear that the number of such theologians is growing rap-
idly, and though it is dangerous to try to predict the shiftings of theological
winds, it appears likely that modern theologies in general will judge—on
Christian grounds—that revelation, truth, and faith are to be found in non-
Christian religions.

The purpose of the foregoing discussions has not been to argue for the particular judgments of any of these theologians, but to illustrate how even in
the very nontraditional proposals being made by today's theologians, the aim
is not to deny traditional Christian faith but to understand more deeply—relative to our time—the reality and the will of God of which we have learned
through the historically conditioned witnessing of the Christian interpreters
who have gone before us. Process theologies, liberation theologies, and theologies affirming religious pluralism (some theologies are all of these!) all challenge traditional convictions and formulations in striking ways. Whether
one accepts or rejects the conclusions of one or more of these positions does
not determine whether one is open to modern theology. Anyone, however,
who rejects such proposals out of hand without a serious effort to understand
how they are offered as implications of the gospel is not only not open to *mod-*

ern theology, but is not open to Christian theology, for such unwillingness to listen is a sign of the anxiety of idolatry. Whether rightly or wrongly, modern Christian theologies are attempts to reaffirm the sovereign grace made manifest to us in Jesus Christ.

SOVEREIGN GRACE AND MODERN THEOLOGY

The recognition that some particular modern theologies are intended to reaffirm the Christian gospel does not directly address the questions concerning the characteristics of modern theology in general. It is these general characteristics, not just some specific approaches and claims, that are disturbing to many Christians. The modern theologians, by contrast, are convinced that the very things that are so disturbing in modern theology are required by the Christian gospel. How can such a disagreement be explained?

The Differing Worlds of Premodern and Modern Theologies

Just what is so disturbing about modern theology? *In general* it is that modern theology has repudiated many features of the premodern world of Christendom that provided believers with a strong sense of security. The more specific points of contrast should be seen in the context of this difference of "worlds."

The premodern world of Christendom was a small world (in both space and time) whose understanding was given by authorities (supposedly) granted by God. This is, of course, a broad generalization, for the many centuries of premodern Christendom included disputes, disagreements, developments, and much that was threatening to human securities. Such facts should be remembered in the presence of all broad generalizations, but they do not deny the point of this generalization. God-given authorities were generally believed in, and they taught that the universe centered spatially upon the earth as the stage for the divine-human drama, which was the sole purpose of creation. Temporally, the whole creation was centered in the event of Jesus Christ. Time extended back but a few thousand years, and any day could be the last. Thus, we human beings were at the center of it all, and the purpose of our lives transcended such problems as hunger, disease, and all such temporary conditions.

These things were known because of Scriptures, creeds, and church authorities, all under divine guidance. Such authorities not only provided sure guidance to the understanding of our place in the universe, but also to right conduct. We humans knew what we should and should not do, for the churches told us, and those churches diligently guarded their authority to keep us on or return us to the path to everlasting reward.

Such a world offers much security. Seen from a modern perspective, it is the security provided by dogmatism and legalism with all of their dehumanizing potential. But in a time of very little education (for the large majority of persons), and a time in which a materially abundant life was not possible for more than a small minority, it may have been as good a world as was possible.

With the success of scientific method—as, in general, we understand that today—that small and secure premodern world was doomed. As understandings of the universe, which the churches had authorized, were shown to be wrong, the churches' authority began to crumble. The slow and painful discovery that the Scriptures, creeds, and councils could be understood to be human and historical and that, whatever role "revelation" and "inspiration" played, they did not leave these "authorities" free from error, prejudice, and historical and cultural relativities required the rethinking of our "world."

Consider the characteristics of modern theology in general: the *recognition* of historical and cultural relativity; the *acceptance* of historical-critical understandings of Scripture and tradition; the entailed reinterpretation of revelation as nonpropositional; the acknowledgment of the unavailability of absolute authorities; the affirmation of the necessity of continual reformulation of doctrinal and moral teachings; the acceptance of pluralism in theology; the recognition of inescapable ambiguity in religious language; the growing awareness of the great complexity of human motivations; and the calling into question of traditional beliefs about the modes of divine activity and of Christian exclusivism. Every characteristic undercuts securities offered by the premodern world.

The Shift of Concern from Heresy to Idolatry

This loss of the security of absolute authorities and correct doctrines is not lamented but praised by modern theology, as is evident in the fact that the premodern critical theological preoccupation with *heresy* has been replaced by concern about *idolatry*. The concept of heresy presupposes a certainty about the truth of one's doctrines. If it can be supposed that the conclusions reached by the official councils regarding the nature, the activity, and the will of God are themselves guaranteed by the guidance of the Holy Spirit and therefore authoritative beyond question, and it is also firmly believed that the teaching of contrary doctrines may lead people into everlasting sufferings, the condemning and punishing of persons who presume to disagree with the official teachings is at least understandable. But when the human and historical character of Scriptures, councils, creeds, doctrines, and theologians becomes manifest, the presuppositions of heresy hunting and suppression become untenable. Indeed, the concepts of "heresy" *and* of "orthodoxy" come to look suspiciously like "idolatry."

When theologians speak of "idolatry" today, they do not have in mind a literal worshiping of a finite object which is called an idol. Actually, when such objects were employed in worship they were intended only to represent or symbolize the deity believed in. "Idolatry" is worshiping, or placing one's basic trust in, or trying to find one's deepest security in "a false god," which is to say, anything other than (the true) God. If, for example, a person is willing to cheat his or her neighbors in order to gain financially, it could be judged that this person trusts more in wealth as a source of security and meaning that in the Deity described in biblical teachings. From the standpoint of biblical faith, this is "idolatry."

Life is full of idolatries, and prominent among them are the more specifically religious idolatries. Whenever religious doctrines, rituals, documents, and the like, are treated as having absolute status—an attribute belonging to God only—there is idolatry. One of the principal critical tasks of theology is to discern when and where religious symbols, doctrines, and so on, have ceased to aid openness to God and have instead become "idols," standing between the believers and God. There is a recognition that the same symbol, ritual, or doctrine—which at one time or for some people facilitated faith—in another time or for other people, or in another time for the *same* people, may have come to impede faith, because those persons are trusting in the symbol (etc.) rather than "hearing" through it.

It might be asked whether this view of "idolatry" is representative of modern theology in general or only of the less rationalistic theologians, for there is assumed here the judgment that *faith* is not essentially believing in doctrines (etc.), but some kind of relationship to God. But that relationship might itself be primarily a matter of "believing," if it is believing in God and not merely believing teachings about God. Even the more rationalistic modern theologians recognize that human beings are more than intellect and that faith is in God rather than in doctrines. They further recognize that doctrinal formulations are ambiguous and historically and culturally relative human constructions. This is not always evident, for theologians often present their positions as if they believed that their own specific conclusions were the truth itself. That, however, is an unfortunate characteristic of the style of some theologians. Modern theologians recognize the limited character of their own teachings and know that theological claims should be made humbly!

Does this iconoclastic character of modern theology ("iconoclasm" is the "smashing of idols") mean that all past doctrinal teachings—such as, for example, the doctrine of the Trinity—are to be repudiated? Certainly not! But it does mean that all such doctrines lose their sacrosanct status. The point is not simply that there must be room for discussion of how such a doctrine is to be interpreted. That has gone on throughout church history. Nor is it simply that one may question the adequacy of any particular formulation of the doctrine, such as that of the Council of Nicaea, whose language in many ways is not ours. Questioning of the doctrine itself—in its many formulations— must be accepted as part of the ongoing task of the church's theologians. Does the doctrine facilitate or impede faith here and now? If or insofar as it does not, why not? Is it that it is misunderstood? Or might it be that its symbolic power in other times and places is no longer operative?

This judgment that the inviolability of certain classical doctrinal formulations has been surrendered by modern theology may be seen to be prejudicial. Although there is no one in the field of modern theology who would condone burning a person at the stake or even depriving one of freedom for denying the doctrine of the Trinity, there are some who, though they manifest most of the characteristics of modern theology, still argue that one *must* affirm God as Father, Son, and Holy Spirit in order to be Christian. The point here is not aimed at those defenders of tradition who offer relevant arguments against criticisms of the traditional doctrine and proposed reformulations of our attempts to portray God. That is entirely consistent with the characteristics of modern theology that we have discussed. The inconsistency arises when some do not reason but *assume* and *assert* those ancient doctrinal formulations *as a given* that is beyond critical discussion. That is to grant to tradition the kind of absolute authority that is no longer tenable—except to those who reject the world of modern theology as a whole. The same is true of those who argue not that the tradition has such authority, but that (in this case) the Nicene formulation of the doctrine of the Trinity is *the* correct interpretation of the teaching of the New Testament. Apart from the fact that there is much room for argument about that judgment, it is again an appeal to a supposed absolute authority of historical human documents.

To illustrate this difference, one may note the suggestion of the depth psychologist C. G. Jung that in the modern Western cultures the Trinity is not an adequate symbolism for wholeness. It is therefore neither satisfactory for expression of the character of divinity nor an effective mediator of reconciliation. Jung judged from the "data" coming from the deeper unconscious that the archetypal symbolism of human wholeness and of divinity has more the character of the fourfold than of the threefold, and that our time is suffering from the absence of the feminine in our symbolisms of deity (Jung 1969, 107–200, 465).

This brief statement of Jung's suggestion is but to touch the tip of an iceberg, but it is sufficient for the purposes of the present illustration. The critical question is how the theologian is to respond to such suggestions. In point of fact, most of today's theologians have not even been interested in Jung's arguments. It is quite impossible for anyone to examine critically all of the proposals being made, and only a minority of today's theologians have been persuaded by Jung's affirmation of the collective unconscious, so only these few would be expected to devote attention to his suggestions of a "Quaternity." Such theologians, however, are taking the questions raised by Jung seriously and exploring their bases and possibilities. Still others have simply argued that because the view is not Trinitarian, it cannot be Christian. The point being urged here is that this last argument is simply not compatible with modern theology. It is the same idolatrous use of tradition noted above. Today one must examine the arguments and the data in order to assess critically whether the formulations or symbolisms of another historical-cultural setting remain the most adequate ways of expressing and interpreting our faith or not. Most modern Christian theologians continue to affirm the doctrine of the Trinity, but they do so on the basis of critical assessment, not by the assumption of a sacrosanct status for orthodox tradition.

Thus the iconoclasm of modern theology does not mean the repudiation of the doctrines of Christian tradition but a continuing critical assessment of how and what they mean today. In these assessments, the burden of proof is on those who argue that basic change should be made, because of the historical fact that the major doctrines of Christian tradition have helped to maintain effective Christian witness in the past. Were that not so, these discussions would not be going on. Christianity is a historical religion. We are dependent upon tradition, though we may also be victimized by it. Tradition is an authority in Christian theology, albeit a relative, not an absolute, authority.

Faith and Grace

In order to see clearly why theology today is so concerned about "idolatry" in this modern sense of the term, judging it to be inevitable and ubiquitous, it is necessary to recognize the dialectical interrelationship of faith and grace. "Faith" is the major traditional Christian term for the human response to "grace." "Grace" is a major traditional Christian term for the character and activity of God as those have been perceived by faith to be embodied in the whole event of Jesus Christ.

"Grace" is a central term in Christian theology, but it is very difficult to clarify its meaning. Its very centrality means that any interpretation is caught up in the whole theology that interprets it. To the degree that one affirms a participationist understanding of faith, grace will be seen as a reality that is understood only experientially, not academically by learning definitions. This is one of the reasons why the word "grace" seems to have lost much of its power in the lives of Christians.

In the basic traditional understanding, "grace" denotes the free, unmerited, and unmeritable *gift* of divine love, acceptance, affirmation toward

God's self-estranged creatures. The term "love" could be seen as a synonym, except that it has an enormous variety of meanings that include powerful attraction and attachment rooted in the *needs* of the "lover." "Grace" signifies an utterly "free gift," which is rooted in "abundance" rather than need or deficiency. It is thus the nature of grace that it cannot be earned, merited, bargained for, or possessed. It is not a substance, a thing in itself, but the very nature of God as "known" by faith. This is not an objective or verifiable knowing. It is "known" only in being trusted. To be knowable objectively and/or verifiable it would have to lose its freedom and its transcendence as God's being toward the creatures. If it could be bargained for, it would be conditional, not free. If it could be possessed, it would not be God's free self-giving.

One way of trying to express the good news, the gospel, then, is to affirm that in the Christ-event it was shown that "we are justified by grace." "Justified" is, however, an even more questionable term today, for it calls up images of the law court that now invite impressions of God as an arbitrary or legalistic Judge—neither of which is very "gracious." These images suggest either the possibility of deserving the acceptance, or of earning it, or of bargaining for it. Grace is thus denied. Therefore, even though the word "justified" is important in the traditions that have carried the gospel in some earlier periods, it is one that must be interpreted, supplemented, and/or replaced today. Words such as "reconciled" and "accepted" have been proposed. Let us say, then, the good news is that we are reconciled or accepted by grace.

Here lies the "offense" of the gospel. It is not our logical reasoning that is offended by affirmations of real or apparent contradictions. Rather it is the self or spirit that is offended by the affirmation that we are accepted by grace, which means that we do not deserve this affirmation by God. The affirmation is a free gift coming from God's graciousness.

Strangely, apart from faith, we do not want such a gift and we cannot believe in it. This is because of the inevitable insecurity of the human situation. Human beings are self-conscious creatures. We are aware of ourselves to a degree that we have not detected in other creatures, and that self-awareness makes possible most of the human achievements. But it is the self-awareness of finite creatures. We know that we are limited, vulnerable, and threatened. We know that we will die, that we will suffer, that we may be lonely, that we may or may not be "good" by some standard, and that our lives may have no meaning. Not everyone articulates these threats, but there is ample evidence that we all experience them. Our lives are, therefore, motivated by efforts to deal with these threats, avoiding death, suffering, and loneliness and seeking ways to persuade ourselves that we are "okay" and that our lives are meaningful. Some persons try instead to keep these deep threats to self hidden from themselves by avoiding the questions and preoccupying themselves with more proximate struggles or diversions. The questions remain, however, for we live them.

Some of those persons who condemn Christian faith do so because they recognize this human motivation of anxious self-protective searching for security and judge that "faith" is one of these self-deceptive security systems. No doubt what passes for Christian faith is often just that. But that is not faith; it is idolatry. If one believes in the reality of God and in eternal life, for example, as a self-deceptive device motivated by anxious self-protectiveness, this is not faith in God's graciousness, it is not trusting in the free gift but clinging to the self's own security systems. This is why so much of what passes for Christianity is so lacking in Christlike characteristics, so ungracious. Idolatrous religion leaves the person captive to the anxieties of the human condition. The motivation remains self-protective and unfree. In this initially inevitable condition, we want the security of knowing that we are approved, of having definitions and rituals that control the source of security. Grace cannot be defined, controlled, or possessed. It can only be trusted. Trusting grace means letting go of one's anxious self-protectiveness, and that is just what the proclamation of the gospel asks us to do. The invitation to faith is no "cop-out." It is the most frightening thing one can be invited to risk—until the risk is taken. Only a gracious God, sovereign grace, makes faith possible. Only faith "knows" that grace is sovereign, which, for Christian faith, is to say that God is.

The difference between faith and unfaith (sin) here can be seen in connection with the questions about Christian belief in eternal life. It is sometimes argued that such a belief is selfish and therefore contrary to faith. It may be in particular cases, but it need not be in itself. The judgment that Christians must believe that death is the last word for humans—lest they be selfish rather than faithful—amounts to saying that there must not be "good news," that is, that because it (eternal life) is something that humans would naturally want, it must not be true. That is surely a strange kind of "gospel." The question is rather one concerning the motivation of the belief. If Christian faith is the utter trust that God is gracious and thus that grace is the essential being for us of that which is ultimate, then it is not possible to suppose that death has the last word. In that case death would be seen as greater than God, and God would not be utterly trustworthy. But faith is that utter trust in God. To affirm belief in eternal life is an expression of that trust, the trust which knows that God is sovereign, that God is greater than death, and therefore that when we die we are yet "in the hands of God." Faith does not, in fact, know what God will do with us, but it does "know" (it trusts utterly) that God will deal with us graciously—and that is enough. To need to know more is to lack trust in God's sovereign graciousness. Thus, *faith's* affirmation of eternal life is not and cannot be selfish. That would be a contradiction.

That there is much idolatrous—rather than faithful—affirmation of such things as eternal life among Christians is no doubt true, and that is why one of the essential tasks of theology is to expose the idolatrous misuses of traditional Christian teachings.

The fact that doctrinal and liturgical formulations are sometimes found to serve idolatry rather than faith does not necessarily mean that they were unsound when proposed. They may well have been very powerful in confronting persons with the affirmation of sovereign graciousness and the challenge to take the risk of faith. Yet, because of the inevitability of anxiety in human existence and of self-protectiveness in human motivations, it is also inevitable that those formulations will be "domesticated" in the life of the churches. In this case, familiarity may not "breed contempt," but it removes the metaphoric shock and facilitates the sense that "of course, I know that." The unrecognized motivation to domesticate effective doctrinal and liturgical forms, namely, the anxious self-protective wish to avoid the risk of trusting utterly in grace, is very powerful and very subtle. Religion as a whole is probably the most subtle way of avoiding the risk of faith *precisely because* it is practiced in the supposition that it is the expression of faith. The answer to this inevitable problem is not the abandonment of religion (as many would urge), but the critical struggle against idolatry. The abandonment of all religiousness, which is to say to surrender all human openness (real as well as false) to the grace of God, even if it were possible, would be but another expression of the human pride that leaves us captive to our anxieties and alienations.

The disturbing characteristics of modern theology, though they have come about in response to the cultural revolutions that led to the modern world, are not to be seen only as accommodations to modernity. They are also, and more importantly, *required by the Christian gospel*. Such, at least, is the judgment of modern theologians.

WORKS CITED

Cobb, J. B., Jr.
  1975   *Christ in a Pluralistic Age*. Philadelphia: Westminster Press.
  1985   "The Religions." In *Christian Theology: An Introduction to Its Traditions and Tasks*. 2d ed., rev. and enl., edited by P. C. Hodgson and R. H. King, 353–76. Philadelphia: Fortress Press.
Cobb, J. B., Jr., and David Ray Griffin.
  1976   *Process Theology: An Introductory Exposition*. Philadelphia: Westminster Press.

Cone, J. H.
    1975   *God of the Oppressed*. A Crossroad Book. New York: Seabury
                      Press.

Hamilton, P.
    1967   *The Living God and the Modern World: Christian Theology Based
                      on the Thought of A. N. Whitehead*. Philadelphia: United
                      Church Press.

Hartshorne, C.
    1967   *A Natural Theology for Our Time*. La Salle, Ill.: Open Court.

Jung, C. G.
    1969   *Psychology and Religion: West and East*. The Collected Works
                      of C. G. Jung, vol. 11. Bollingen Series XX, 2d ed. Princeton:
                      Princeton University Press.

Ogden, S. M.
    1963   *The Reality of God and Other Essays*. New York: Harper &
                      Row.

Rahner, K.
    1966   *Theological Investigations*. Translated by Karl-H. Kruger. Vol.
                      5. Baltimore: Helicon Press.

Smith, W. C.
    1981   *Towards a World Theology: Faith and the Comparative History of
                      Religion*. Philadelphia: Westminster Press.

Tillich, P.
    1951   *Systematic Theology*. Vol. 1. Chicago: University of Chicago
                      Press.

    1966   *The Future of Religions*. Edited by J. C. Brauer. New York:
                      Harper & Row.

Wall, J. M., ed.
    1981   *Theologians in Transition*. The Christian Century "How My
                      Mind Has Changed" Series. New York: Crossroad.

INDEX

14.95
L 3-7

Understanding
Modern
Theology I

UNDERSTANDING MODERN THEOLOGY I

*Cultural Revolutions
and New Worlds*

JEFFERY HOPPER

FORTRESS PRESS   PHILADELPHIA

Page 106: Illustration is reproduced from *New Introductory Lectures on Psychoanalysis* by Sigmund Freud, translated by James Strachey, with the permission of W. W. Norton & Company, Inc. Copyright © 1965, 1964 by James Strachey. Copyright 1933 by Sigmund Freud. Copyright renewed 1961 by W. J. H. Sprott. Further acknowledgment is given to Sigmund Freud Copyrights Ltd., The Institute of Psycho-Analysis and The Hogarth Press for permission to quote from *The Standard Edition of the Complete Psychological Works of Sigmund Freud* translated and edited by James Strachey.

Pages 131 and 135: From Alfred M. Perry, "The Growth of the Gospels," in *The Interpreter's Bible*, vol. 7. Nashville: Abingdon Press, 1951. Reprinted by permission.

Biblical quotations, unless otherwise noted, are from the Revised Standard Version of the Bible, copyright 1946, 1952, © 1971, 1973 by the Division of Christian Education of the National Council of the Churches of Christ in the U.S.A., and are used by permission.

COPYRIGHT © 1987 BY FORTRESS PRESS

All rights reserved. No part of this publication may be reproduced, stored in a retrieval system, or transmitted in any form or by any means, electronic, mechanical, photocopying, recording, or otherwise, without the prior permission of the publisher, Fortress Press.

Library of Congress Cataloging-in-Publication Data

Hopper, Jeffery, 1930–
   Understanding modern theology.

   Bibliography: p.
   1. Theology, Doctrinal—History—Modern period,
1500–   . I. Title.
BT27.H67   1986   230'.09'03   86–45210
ISBN 0–8006–1929–3

2539F86   Printed in the United States of America   1–1929